Teaching with The Norton Anthology of Poetry

FOURTH EDITION

A Guide for Instructors

THE EDITORS

Margaret Ferguson
COLUMBIA UNIVERSITY

Mary Jo Salter
MOUNT HOLYOKE COLLEGE

Jon Stallworthy
OXFORD UNIVERSITY

Teaching with The Norton Anthology of Poetry

FOURTH EDITION

A Guide for Instructors

Mark Jeffreys
UNIVERSITY OF ALABAMA AT BIRMINGHAM

Debra Fried
CORNELL UNIVERSITY

W · W · NORTON & COMPANY
New York · London

The text of this book is composed in Electra
with the display set in Bernhard Modern.
Composed by Crane Typesetting Service, Inc.
Manufacturing by Haddon Craftsmen.

ISBN 0-393-96923-1 (pbk.)

W. W. Norton & Company, Inc., 500 Fifth Avenue, New York, N.Y. 10110
http://www.wwnorton.com

W. W. Norton & Company Ltd., 10 Coptic Street, London WC1A 1PU

1 2 3 4 5 6 7 8 9 0

Contents

III. Topics

Introduction: The Anthology as Textbook

This Course Guide is designed to suggest ways of using *The Norton Anthology of Poetry*, Fourth Edition, as a textbook in introductory courses in poetry. An anthology cannot possess the neat pedagogic order of a syllabus, in part because an anthology has at least two sets of authors: the poets who, over many centuries, wrote the selections, and the editors who chose and arranged them. In *The Last Gentlemen*, Walker Percy nicely observes this double parentage: "From the anthology there arose a subtler smell, both exotic and businesslike, of the poet's disorder, his sweats and scribblings, and of the office order of the professor and his sweet ultimate ink." We hope that this Guide will be both exotic and businesslike enough to be of value to a third set of authors: the instructors who will select and rearrange the poems—anthologize them, we might say—for their classroom uses. It is intended not as a handbook of classroom procedures, but as a reference book that will enable teachers to find their way around in the anthology and to choose, group, and discuss poems in diverse ways.

Using this Guide

The Norton Anthology of Poetry arranges poems chronologically by author, an ordering designed to make it easy to locate an individual poet, and also to give students a rough idea of the historical sequence and the evolution of poetic forms, devices, and subjects. But most of us who teach poetry to undergraduates will wish to impress on our students that a literary tradition can be understood in ways other than by proceeding from Cædmon's "Hymn" straight through to the poems of Cynthia Zarin. Students will certainly be more astute readers of Cædmon's "Hymn" if they read it in the context of the other Old English poetry in the anthology, but they are likely to enjoy it more, and to see more point in studying it, if they also discover its position in the long tradition of hymns in English. And reading hymns can introduce the formal linkages among hymns, ballads, and spirituals. Discussing the use of common meter in these forms can, in turn, introduce students to the variations on that traditional and popular measure in, say, Blake and Dickinson. And if it seems a long way from Cædmon to Blake and Dickinson, a consideration of such themes as God, praise, faith, and doubt will tie both of the later poets to Cædmon once again. Conversely, at the small end of our historical telescope, a poem such as Zarin's "The Ant Hill" gains immeasurably when seen in the context of other poems, recent and ancient, that feature images of childhood, of recurring seasonal change, of the interweaving of animal and human rhythms. Thus "The Ant Hill" is cited at numerous points in this Guide—for instance in section 16.6, "Seasons and Seasonal Change"; section 15.3, "Children and Childhood"; section 16.4, "Animals"; section 7.3B, "Meditation, Confession, and Invitation"; and section 3.4, "Closure." Many poems will reappear in this way under a number of headings, usually grouped once with poems that have similar structures or that exemplify similar features of versification, then grouped again with poems that concern similar subjects or that raise related issues in the teaching of poetry, such as diction or tone. Other poems will not be listed in the Guide at all. For maximal use, we have listed only those poems common to both the regular and shorter editions of *The Norton Anthology of Poetry*, Fourth Edition.

Since all examples in this guide are meant as suggestions, there is nothing peremptory, final, or exhaustive about these groupings of poems, or about the arrangement of the lists. Each group can occupy any desired amount of time in a course: a passing reference, a class section, a week, or even several weeks. While we have arranged the Guide according to a rough sequential logic of classroom presentation, we have also suggested a variety of other ways in which a poetry course might be organized. The Guide therefore consists of three major categories of material: "Components," which surveys formal and rhetorical issues such as meter, rhyme, stanzas, narrative, closure, fixed forms, figuration, diction, and audience; "Traditions and Counter-Traditions," which recontextualizes the poems in terms not of form but of allusion, influence, intertextuality, parody, dialect, gender, marginality, and so forth; and "Topics," which simply offers a broad diversity of thematic clusters, from "Times of Day" to "Fidelity and Infidelity" to "Racial and Ethnic Identity" to "The World

Beyond." Some instructors will want to begin a course by covering the basic formal terminology of poetry, while others will prefer to establish say, a matrix of social themes and use the formal sections in "Components" as resources to be dipped into when useful or necessary. Examining the range of responses poets have expressed to something that students have experienced for themselves (the seasons, city life, love, solitude) is one good way to introduce questions of structure and language. For instance, what different views of love do we find in different genres? How do poems about love draw upon the poets' inventiveness in language, in comparisons, and in figurations? What different modes of address, even what sorts of metrical innovations and conventions, are illustrated by poems about love? Alternatively, asking students to read and compare poems about animals can be a way of introducing them to the significance of patterns and rhetorical schemes: Why does Blake confront the tiger by asking a battery of questions, while Shelley addresses the skylark by testing a series of likenesses? A course that began with a selection of poems written by members of marginalized groups, such as " 'Peasant' and 'Blue-Collar' Poets" (12.1) or "African-American Poets" (12.3), could start by raising the question of poetry's own central or marginal status among the dominant (elite?) culture, and perhaps move to the relations between the powers of poetic voice and the dominant culture's "Influence and Intertextuality" (9). Because each section of the Guide implies issues that are raised more explicitly in other sections, an instructor should find it simple to select and arrange lists from each section in the order that will best suit the design of a particular course. In most cases, the lists contain more poems than any instructor will wish to teach in a single course; we expect that in class discussions instructors will focus on only some of the poems from a list, although they may want also to bring students' attention to other poems as supplementary reading, or for essay assignments, in-class reports, and other exercises.

The most challenging task in preparing a course may be the job of reshuffling these lists into a coherent syllabus; uncharitably enough, this task is left to the instructor. We hope that the lists will suggest other possible groupings and prompt the invention of new ways to introduce poetry to beginning students. But of course these lists are not innocent: the mere act of categorizing a poem imposes interpretation on it, and urges a method of teaching it as well. One principle this Guide implicitly favors is that it is more effective to compare poems than to teach them in isolation: two poems make a better lesson than one. The reasons for this bias are obvious, perhaps, but worth rehearsing anyway. On the simplest pedagogic level, beginning students who may be somewhat hesitant to contribute to a discussion about one poem will often find it easier to respond when they are asked in a specific way to compare two poems. More important, teaching poems in conjunction is one way of encouraging students to reflect on how poems may engage the history of poetry; to understand that poets do not write as though no poems had ever been written before, but that poems may be occasioned both by a personal need of the poet and by other poems. Poems are often implicit acts of comparison (sometimes in homage, sometimes in rivalry, most often in an uneasy combination of the two) to other poems and other poets. To train students to read poetry, therefore, entails, in part, to train them to read certain poems while keeping certain other poems in mind. Put simply, students really begin learning about poetry when most poems they read remind them in some way of some other poems they have read. We have tried to suggest affinities among selections in the anthology that will encourage fruitful and provocative cross-referencing of poems on the part of students.

All but a few of the lists are headed by a brief paragraph that offers some basic definitions of the issues or poetic features highlighted by the list and that explains the rationale for the grouping, when it isn't obvious. These introductory paragraphs sketch some possible approaches to teaching the poems on the list, usually in the form of a series of related questions. In some cases, you might pose these questions to yourself as you prepare a lesson; in other cases, you might address these questions to the class in order to focus discussion, or you might use them as a basis for writing assignments. Sometimes these headnotes point to other lists that raise related issues. The implicit view behind such cross-references is that there are no purely formal issues in teaching poetry any more than there are purely thematic ones. It can be just as effective to teach elegies by asking the class to think about such matters as diction and closure as by explicitly considering questions of death and loss as poetic subjects.

The bulk of this Guide is made up of questions that follow many of the individual poems in the lists. In general, these questions are designed to link each of the poems in specific ways to the concerns outlined in the headnote. Most of the questions are of the sort an instructor might address to undergraduates taking their first poetry course. We expect, though, that each instructor will find some of these questions more basic and pedagogically useful, but find others more suitable as guides to the teacher's own preparation than as inquiries for a class to explore. We hope that even those questions (and there are bound to be some) that some instructors find tendentious, picayune, or wrongheaded will be useful in helping them come to clearer decisions about how best to teach the poems. (An instructor who poses one of the questions in this Guide that he or she judges least helpful and asks the class to consider why it is not a good question might well end up with a better lesson than would be sparked by a better question.) The questions vary in focus, degree of specificity, and scope. Since, again, a principal goal has been to help the instructor teach one poem in terms of others, "compare" is probably the most frequent suggestion in this Guide. Sometimes the questions try to suggest ways of thinking about the progression of a poem, how it moves from first line to last, how the opening stanzas prepare for the closing ones. For the most part we have asked questions that will require the student to look carefully at the text, to read and reread, to gauge the effect of a particular word or line in terms of its relation to other parts of the poem or even to other poems. Sweeping, vague questions can lead away from the poem at hand: "How does the speaker feel about all this?" or "What is the tone of this poem?" or "What is this poem about?" are less reliably effective questions than simpler, more-specific ones that you would probably have to ask somewhere along the line anyway in guiding a class toward the larger answers. We prefer to ask, "How does this choice of word suggest what the speaker feels about all this?" or "What does the way this line is repeated tell us about the tone of this poem?" or even "What does the title of this poem suggest that it is about, and is the title accurate?" Such questions should have the initial effect, at least, of forcing students to read poems more slowly, and to treat these curious, patterned, unfamiliar structures of words with attention and patience.

From time to time the headnotes suggest an exercise designed to teach the topic exemplified in the list. Some of these exercises involve revising parts of a poem to examine the effects of changes in certain poetic forms or devices; others involve imitating a poetic pattern or technique. Occasionally, brief suggestions for exercises in the teaching of an individual poem are listed with the questions for that poem, not in the headnote.

Poems and exercises linked to *The Norton Poetry Workshop on CD-ROM* are marked "CD-ROM Link." The CD-ROM provides students with additional exercises and important contextual material on thirty poets included in *The Norton Anthology of Poetry*, Fourth Edition.

Dealing with Student Preconceptions

The lists, headnotes, and questions in this Guide offer very little in the way of historical or biographical information; the footnotes and brief biographies in the anthology itself provide most of the essential commentary of this nature. That the answers to most of the questions a beginning student is likely to be concerned with lie within the poems themselves (although that "within" demarcates a blurry borderline) seems to us one of the most important things a teacher can demonstrate in an introductory course in poetry. The goal of such a course should be to equip our students not as scholars but as readers of poetry. Beginning students, in our experience, can be all too eager to defer to some vague historical difference or to invent some esoteric authority to account for what seems to them the strangeness or subversiveness, the unfamiliar obliquity or uncomfortable bluntness of poems. If the opinion they take a poem to express about love, or old age, or religion, or loneliness does not concur with their own opinions or with what they take to be current opinions, many students will appeal to some principle of cultural or historical relativism: "That's the way they used to think about these things." One way for the instructor to keep from catering to this tendency is to take advantage of the freedom this anthology grants to teach poems from any period of English or American poetry in any sequence. Most of the lists in this Guide try to suggest the pedagogic benefits of that freedom. You can help students to see the inadequacy of the notion that the difficulty of poetry lies chiefly in its outmoded dress and antiquated ways of thinking and feeling by having them discover that poems written ten years ago may be every bit as odd, bristly, and formidable as poems written four hundred years ago. Just as important, teaching links between poems can help students to discover the relevance of those centuries-old poems themselves.

By these caveats we don't mean to imply, of course, that there are no differences in the challenges poems of different periods will present to students, or that they should be encouraged to ignore such differences. Even if, as Auden said, poetry makes nothing happen, it does not follow that nothing happens to poetry. The tendency of beginning students, however, to appeal to history as the sole, or at least primary, agent of the changes that make poetry hard to read is especially puzzling when you consider that if students have been told anything about poetry before they take up the subject in college, it is that poetry is timeless, inviolable, a separate realm in which "universal" human feelings can take such different shapes and be sounded in such different tones that it is hard to be certain they are the same feelings at all.

Teaching poems by authors who belong to minority or ethnic groups or who for some reason are placed outside of the group of white males whose modes of response are usually classed as "universal human feelings" is another way to combat the myth that poetry is an escape from history. Poetry is a part of history, as history is inevitably part of poetry. As Hartley observed, "The past is a foreign country; they do things differently there." The challenge is to allow students to discover this for themselves, without isolating each group and each historical period as hopelessly alien and yet without encouraging the appropriation of all poets and poems to the students' own worldview in the guise of universal, transcendent themes.

ACKNOWLEDGMENTS

We would like to thank Julia Reidhead, Anna Karvellas, and Tara Parmiter at Norton for the opportunity to produce this Guide and for all their patient assistance. Thanks also to Ron Schuchard for his support, and to Flowers Braswell, Steve Glosecki, Ted Haddin, Bridget Keegan, Nancy Miller, and Elaine Whitaker for their specific suggestions regarding format changes and classroom exercises.

I. Components

CHAPTER 1

Versification

1.1 The Poetic Line

That poetry is written in lines is one of the most fundamental, but also one of the most complex, things about it. One good way of introducing this topic—and perhaps the course itself—would be to prepare a list illustrating the wide spectrum of possibilities for the poetic line that the anthology offers. The instructor might compile this list, or have students browse through the anthology, collecting samples of lines they find peculiar or interesting. Most students will recognize **Wordsworth's** "I wandered lonely as a cloud," for instance, as the kind of thing a line of poetry tends to sound like, but it is important for them to realize that " 'Were you happy?' 'Yes.' 'And are you still as happy?' 'Yes. And you?' " in **Browning's** "A Toccata of Galuppi's" is also a line of poetry, as is "Six o'clock" in **Eliot's** "Preludes" or "Methinks" in **Thoreau's** "I Am a Parcel of Vain Strivings Tied." As a group, these poems suggest how wide and colorful is the spectrum of what poetic lines can look and sound like. An allied exercise: select a few short prose paragraphs and have the students break them up into lines to make them look and sound as much like what they consider a poem (a free verse poem, most likely) to look and sound like, and explain the reasons for their choices. This is a useful exercise to do while studying enjambed and end-stopped lines as well (see section 1.1C).

A. *Illustrating the Variety of Poetic Lines*

By beginning with a group of poems that feature lines of varying lengths, you can both illustrate the effect of such variations within a poem and assign these poems as practice exercise in scansion. What is the effect of very short lines? How do short lines tend to isolate and emphasize the words in the line? How do longer lines bring attention to the grouping of words and sounds in the line? Even before you go into detail about the differences between metered verse and free verse, you might ask students about some general differences between the varied line lengths in poems with regular meter and poems in more open or "free" forms.

Cædmon's "Hymn": Call the students' attention to the split presentation of the original Anglo-Saxon lines. How are the two parts of each line linked more closely to each other, rhythmically and contextually, than to the preceding or following half-lines?
Skelton, "To Mistress Margaret Hussey": What is the effect of isolating in a line of its own each of the woman's praiseworthy attributes?
Donne, "Song"
Herrick, "An Ode for Him ('Go and catch a falling star')"
Herbert, "The Collar"
Wordsworth, "Ode: Intimations of Immortality"
R. Browning, "Home-Thoughts, From Abroad"
Thoreau, "I Am a Parcel of Vain Strivings Tied"
Hardy, "The Convergence of the Twain"
S. Crane, From *The Black Riders and Other Lines*: Crane insisted that these pieces be called "lines," not "poems." How does it change our expectations of these texts to think of them as "just" lines, rather than as poems? And, since poems are composed of lines and lines of phrases and individual words, why do you think that Crane stuck with "lines" and did not go so far as to call them simply "words"? Does "lines" seem a more accurate term here? Why?
Williams, "Poem" and "Asphodel, That Greeny Flower": In "Asphodel, That Greeny Flower," where do the lines begin—at each return to the left margin or with each indented phrase? You might ask students to consider the subjects and rhythms of the phrases to see if they seem to "start over again" each time the print returns to the left margin. More generally, is a line defined more by the scrolling return of the text down the page or by the visual isolation of phrases by any white space, vertical or horizontal?
Lawrence, "Snake": What sorts of energies are released when very short lines are set next to very long ones?
Moore, "The Fish" and "The Mind Is an Enchanting Thing": What happens if the lines in these poems are read with an emphatic pause

at each line break? What changes then if they are read without attention to their breaks at all? How is the rhyme scheme of "The Fish" dependent on the presentation of the lines to be heard?

Warren, "Masts at Dawn": What makes these long lines rhythmically different from paragraphs of prose?

Auden, "In Praise of Limestone": Compare the effect of lines that seem to stand on their own ("They were right, my dear, all those voices were right," line 60), and lines that are a composite of logical or grammatical segments that started before them and continue after them ("Need to be altered.' [Intendant Caesars rose and," line 54). What kinds of interesting mistakes or incongruities will arise if you try to read such lines as a logical whole ("Remains comprehensible: to become a pimp," line 40)?

R. Lowell, "For the Union Dead"

Baraka, "In Memory of Radio"

Boland, "That the Science of Cartography Is Limited": Do the lines that stand alone seem more forceful than those grouped in stanzas? *CD-ROM Link

B. *Phrases and Pauses (see "Versification")*

The subtleties of the poetic line include the use of internal pauses (caesurae) between phrases. These pauses can work to break the monotony of highly regular meter, to loosen the sense of the line as a tightly knit unit, or, conversely, to more tightly bind a line by balancing two phrases that generate perpetual tension as a kind of centripetal force (as in this well-known line from **Yeats's** "The Second Coming": "Things fall apart; the centre cannot hold").

Dickinson, #745 ("Renunciation—is a piercing Virtue—"]: Dickinson's poetry is renowned for its distinctive and sometimes puzzling use of dashes, both in place of standard punctuation and at points where no punctuation would be expected. Are the pauses forced by these dashes, as in line 3, "A Presence—for an Expectation," more emphatic than the pauses felt at the ends of her lines? And what of lines that also end with an abrupt dash, as all lines except line 2 of this poem do? Note the parallelism in the phrasing set off by the dashes in lines 1 and 3. Does the placing of the pauses rhythmically equate the opening phrase of each line ("Renunciation" and "A Presence") despite their dissimilarity in number of syllables and patterns of stress?

W. C. Williams, "Asphodel, That Greeny Flower"

Ondaatje, From "Rock Bottom," "(Ends of the Earth)": Are the line breaks in this poem merely coincident with the pauses natural to the syntax? In line 5, "lost without your company, you," how does the isolation of the monosyllable "you" after a late caesura weight the line to suggest a greater loss than simply "lost without your company" would alone or even than "lost without you, your company"?

Lee, "Persimmons": How does this poem use pauses, especially medial caesurae, to re-create the sense of both difference and dialogue between Chinese and English, Asian and Western strands of the speaker's cultural heritage, and men and women? If you are teaching a class in which several ethnicities and at least two or three different first languages are represented, you might have students in small, mixed groups try drafting a few lines of their own in which phrases in one language are set opposite their equivalents in another tongue, the idea being to try and build a short dialogue of cultures within a series of lines. Note how this repetitive pattern builds its own rhythms, distinct from everyday speech, into the lines, and how the pauses become gaps that are suggestive, as in Lee's poem, of what is lost in translation. Encourage the students to ask each other for the names of words they would most like to know in each other's native tongue. *CD-ROM Link

C. *Enjambment and End-Stopped Lines (see "Versification")*

The lists below isolate poems in which either enjambment or end-stopping is dominant. Most poems will combine these two sorts of lineation, sometimes in ways that respond closely to the poem's content. In **Keats's** "On First Looking into Chapman's Homer," for instance, the first eight lines, corresponding to the period before the poet read Homer in Chapman's translation, are end-stopped; the eye-opening experience of reading Chapman releases the poem into a more fluid pattern of enjambment. As an exercise to clarify the difference between enjambed and end-stopped lines, choose one of the poems from the list of end-stopped lines, revise it by breaking it up into shorter lines with strong enjambments, and ask students to discuss the changes in meaning and emphasis that result. For instance, relineate **Smart's** "Jubilate Agno ('For I will consider my Cat Jeoffry')" as **W. C. Williams** might have written it, so that lines 749–50 become something like this:

For he can jump
over a stick, which

is patience upon
proof
positive. For he
can spraggle

upon waggle at
the word
of command.

In a strongly enjambed line, the meaning of the line changes, sometimes slightly, sometimes greatly, when the reader discovers the syntactic continuation of the line in the next one. For instance, in **Blake's** "To the Evening Star," line 8 ends with the injunction to the star to "Let thy west wind sleep on"; line 9 reveals that "sleep on" here is not an idiomatic phrase meaning "continue to sleep, keep on sleeping," but rather requires completion by an object for the preposition "on": "sleep on / The lake." A strong enjambment may make a single word straddle two lines, momentarily isolating the elements that make up the word, as in **Williams's** "The Red Wheelbarrow." And syntax may leap across a stanza break, as throughout **Moore's** "The Fish" and **Zarin's** "The Ant Hill." In the poems listed here the enjambments are particularly strong or noticeable, or especially important to the poem's tone and meaning. An exercise: have students relineate parts of poems from this list to eliminate as many ambiguities or possible confusions as they can, which may mean making the lines as end-stopped as possible. What new meanings and openings for interpretation does this rearrangement introduce into the poem?

Milton, From *Paradise Lost*, Book 1 [The Invocation]

Blake, "To the Evening Star": Ending a line with "the," as Blake does line 5, is a rarity in poetry before the modern period; compare the effect of this line break here and in a later instance such as Moore's "The Fish" or Zarin's "The Ant Hill."

R. Browning, "My Last Duchess": What features of the duke's language make it flow so naturally from one line to the next that it is almost impossible to hear that the poem is written in rhymed couplets?

Robinson, "Miniver Cheevy"

W. C. Williams, "The Red Wheelbarrow" and "Poem"

Moore, "The Fish"

Brooks, "We Real Cool": As a collective exercise, have a student relineate this poem on the board so that the line breaks follow the punctuation (i.e., "We real cool. / We left school," etc.). Ask the class how this changes the poem and its focus. Most classes will discuss their way to noticing that the "We" speaking the poem is deemphasized by the change; point out (if they have not) that Brooks's enjambments not only focus our attention on that "We" but also on its absence in the final line, following "die soon." Why is that absence important to the meaning of the poem? *CD-ROM Link

Hecht, "The Ghost in the Martini": How does Hecht use enjambment to create a kind of comic timing in his lines?

Boland, "That the Science of Cartography Is Limited": Compare to Moore's and Zarin's enjambments—how is Boland's technique similar? Can students pick out any differences in her effects? More generally, this raises the question of whether enjambment is always used for similar purposes or to similar effect. *CD-ROM Link

Zarin, "The Ant Hill": How does the enjambment, especially crossing between stanzas, build a kind of stepping-stone suspense or expectation in this poem that otherwise emphasizes the mundane repetitiveness of the seasons of childhood, "of school, of being sent to bed, of being / told to put the book down"?

Whereas enjambment may be used in rhymed and metered verse to modulate the regularity of the prosody with a counter rhythm that pulls the reader more fluidly from line to line (see the **Browning** example above), end-stopping is a different sort of achievement in the selections from **Smart, Whitman,** and **Corso** below. Without a metrical count to adhere to, these poets can extend their lines as long as they want to, or as long as the line needs to be to complete its unit of thought. Thus the challenge becomes one of using end-stopped lines to arrest or pause the free-flow of the syntax, creating a larger, sweeping, but still noticeable rhythmical unit. How do **Smart** and **Whitman** both try to imitate, and thus allude to, the feel of biblical poetry?

Tichborne, "Tichborne's Elegy": If you relineated this poem so that it contained frequent enjambments, how would its impact be diluted? It might be instructive to compare this poem of a young life destroyed with Brooks's "We Real Cool" (*CD-ROM Link). Here the end-stopping of balanced, antithetical, paradoxical lines is as effective in focusing the readers' attention on the bitter irony of the situation as the enjambment of her poem is in drawing our attention to the abrupt excision of Brooks's doomed speaker.

Smart, From "Jubilate Agno ('For I will consider my Cat Jeoffry')"

Whitman, "Song of Myself" and "Out of the Cradle Endlessly Rocking": All of the selections from Whitman are good examples of end-stopped poetry. How does Whitman's end-stopping serve his needs as a list-maker, as a poet who tries to get the whole world into his poetry? Notice that each rolling line introduces a new idea, category, or image and that immediately succeeding images are often drawn from opposite extremes of the same spectrum, be it social, geographical, or seasonal, so that the two lines between them imply all the intermediate range of that spectrum. Thus the silence of the firm stop at the end of these long lines signifies even without stating. It can be rewarding for teacher and students alike when a class begins to understand the variety of roles that prosodic choices play in the way poems actually mean. *CD-ROM Link

Corso, "Marriage": Although there is often no punctuation mark at the end of the lines, each line completes a single unit of thought or completes a single item in a list. As an exercise, you might ask students to compare Corso's unpunctuated lines to the punctuated lines of Whitman. Also, how do these extended, end-stopped lines of Corso's allude to Whitman?

1.2 Meter and Scansion

A. *Iambic Pentameter (See "Versification")*

A large proportion of poems in English, and hence a large proportion of poems in this anthology, are in iambic pentameter. The list for this section includes only a small portion of the anthology's selections that might be used to illustrate the development of pentameter from the fourteenth century to the twentieth century. Also, this list includes only poems that are in iambic pentameter; poems in other pentameter forms can be found in section 1.2E, "Meters Other Than Iambic." In reading poems from this sample, you might ask your students what historical changes they can detect in the meter's rigor or tautness, from the bouncing, chiefly end-stopped couplets of **Chaucer** to the colloquial, slackened lines of **Frost.**

Chaucer, From *The Canterbury Tales*, "The Pardoner's Prologue and Tale": The Epilogue (lines 631–68) is particularly good for illustrating the flexibility of Chaucer's pentameters. How does Chaucer make the pentameter line serve for the Pardoner's slimy sales pitch (lines 631–57),the Host's invective (lines 658–67), the Knight's call for reconciliation (lines 670–79), and the narrator's exposition (lines 668–69, 672–73, and 680)? *CD-ROM Link

Surrey, "Wyatt Resteth Here"

Tichborne, "Tichborne's Elegy"

Spenser, From *The Faerie Queene*, Book 1: How does the final hexameter (six-foot line) of the Spenserian stanza make the prevailing five-foot line more audible? Compare Shelley's use of this stanza in his elegy for Keats, "Adonais," and Keats's adaptation of the Spenserian stanza to a different kind of storytelling in "The Eve of St. Agnes."

Campion, "My Sweetest Lesbia"

Donne, "The Good-Morrow"

Jonson, "Inviting a Friend to Supper" and "To Penshurst"

Herrick, "The Argument of His Book"

Milton, "On Shakespeare"

Bradstreet, "The Author to Her Book"
Taylor, "Meditation 8 ('I Kenning through astronomy divine')"
Gray, "Elegy Written in a Country Churchyard"
Wordsworth, "Ode: Intimations of Immortality" and "Elegaic Stanzas": Iambic-pentameter lines are interwoven with shorter lines in the varied stanza forms of the ode. Compare the stanzas that end with pentameter lines (4, 5, 6, 8, and 11) with those that do not: how does iambic pentameter become associated with some form of stability or permanence? Why does pentameter become the dominant meter in the final stanza?
Landor, "Dying Speech of an Old Philosopher"
Shelley, "Ode to the West Wind": Compare the use of pentameter throughout this ode (written in terza rima) to its occasional use in Wordworth's "Ode: Intimations of Immortality."
Emerson, "The Rhodora"
Tennyson, Songs from *The Princess*, "Tears, Idle Tears" and "Now Sleeps the Crimson Petal"
Arnold, "The Scholar-Gypsy": What is the effect of the trimeter lines around which these otherwise pentameter stanzas pivot?
Meredith, From "Modern Love," 48 ("Their sense is with their senses all mixed in")
Yeats, "Adam's Curse" and "The Second Coming"
Robinson, "Richard Cory"
Frost, "The Most of It" and "The Gift Outright"
Pound, "Portrait d'une Femme"
Owen, "Strange Meeting"
Bogan, "Song for the Last Act"
Hope, "Australia"
Merrill, "The Victor Dog"
Gunn, "On the Move"
Hill, From "An Apology for the Revival of Christian Architecture in England," "9. The Laurel Axe"

B. Blank Verse (See "Versification)

In "The Verse," his preface to *Paradise Lost,* **Milton** argues that unrhymed iambic pentameter, or "English heroic verse," is productive of "true musical delight; which consists only in apt numbers, fit quantity of syllables, and the sense variously drawn out from one verse into another, not in the jingling sound of like endings, a fault avoided by the learned ancients both in poetry and in all good oratory." Beyond Milton's claim to "musical delight," however, the selections listed below from **Wordsworth, Tennyson, Browning,** and **Frost,** among others, also raise the vexed question of how closely blank verse approximates "the natural rhythms of spoken English," as suggested by Jon Stallworthy in his essay on versification. Is it merely convention (for instance, its long history in dramatic verse) that seems to make blank verse so suitable for creating a meditative or speaking voice, or is it this meter's reflection of or adaptation to English rhythms and intonations that fosters the impression that an individual voice is speaking, with unrehearsed hesitations, spontaneous questions, and unfolding qualifications? An exercise that may bring this debate alive is to have students listen to spoken English (in conversations, lectures, news broadcasts, etc.) for a week and try to detect passages or lines that approximate iambic pentameter ("I can't believe I have a test today," "Let's leave that topic for tomorrow's class," "The congressman could not be reached for comment"). Have them submit two or three such overheard pentameters (or perhaps bits of colloquial conversation as represented in a novel or play) along with two or three they have made up; the point is to make the invented lines sound overheard, then see if the class can tell the difference. Or have the students compile all the lines submitted by the class and arrange them to make a dramatic monologue out of them.

Another exercise: have students recast into iambic pentameter a short poem in another meter. How does the speaker's tone change with this transformation? For instance, expanding the clipped lines of **Dickinson's** #49 ("I never lost as much but twice"), turns the poem into more of a sober, meditative account of loss than a riddling cry of pain, and requires the reviser to fill out with adjectives the curt, epigrammatic phrases ("door of God"). Perhaps **Emily Brontë** (see "Remembrance"), but never **Emily Dickinson,** could have written this version (our additions or changes are bracketed): "Twice have I stood, a beggar, [all in rags], I never lost as much, [except for] twice, And that was in the [unforgiving] sod. Twice have I stood, a beggar, [all in rags], Before the [shut, unyielding] door of God."

Poems in blank verse that aspire to a conversational informality and naturalness include:

Wordsworth, Selection from *The Prelude*, Book I
Coleridge, "Frost at Midnight"
Frost, "Mending Wall," "The Wood-pile," "Birches," "Directive"

Another question: to what subjects does unrhymed iambic pentameter seem best suited? How does the absence of rhyme put pressure on other formal features (syntax, enjambment, repetition, rhetorical structures) to do the job of annotating words (defining, qualifying, linking to other instances of the word and other words in the poem)? Or of associating words and units of thought in the way that rhyme associates them in other pentameter poems, such as in heroic couplets? How do the looser five-beat forms of twentieth-century poetry (**Stevens, R. Lowell**) allude to the blank-verse tradition even while deviating from it?

Milton, *Paradise Lost*, Book 1, lines 1–26: Freeing his poetry from what he called "the troublesome and modern bondage of rhyming," Milton arrived at what to Samuel Johnson seemed "verse only to the eye." What did Johnson mean, and was he right?

Blake, "To the Evening Star": Set against conventional sonnets, this blank-verse sonnet is a good poem in which to test what happens when rhyme is omitted from a verse genre that is normally rhymed.

Wordsworth, "Lines Composed a Few Miles Above Tintern Abbey" and selection from *The Prelude*, Book I

Coleridge, "Frost at Midnight"

Tennyson, "Ulysses" and "Tithonus": How does Tennyson make these two mythical figures—one heroically yearning, the other eternally weary—sound quite different although they speak in the same meter? *CD-ROM Link

Browning, "Fra Lippo Lippi": What is the metrical effect of the snatches of song Fra Lippo interjects? By interposing moments of strongly stressed rhythm, do they encourage our belief that Fra Lippo's speech is natural and spontaneous, rather than designed to seem so through skillful manipulation of meter?

Whitman, "When I Heard the Learn'd Astronomer": A poem not in blank verse but useful for teaching it: why does the last line fall into iambic pentameter? The meditative tone and the way some of Whitman's lines flirt with the five-beat tradition make this poem a good basis for a versification exercise: have students rewrite this poem as blank verse and account for what happens. For instance, recasting the first line as "When once I heard the learn'd astronomer" brings out all four syllables of the last word with a clarity much greater than in Whitman's line. Arguably, it also underlines the word's etymology (astron, star + nomos, law) as the more blurred, vernacular pronunciation of Whitman's line does not. Which of Whitman's extravagances become pruned by rewriting the poem in blank verse? How does his voice, and the very nature of his protest here, change when it speaks in iambic pentameter? (An even more revealing assignment for advanced students, as much about poetic voice as about meter: rewrite "When I Heard the Learn'd Astronomer" in blank verse as Wordsworth, Browning, and Frost would have done it.)

Frost, "Mending Wall," "The Wood-pile," and "Birches"

Edward Thomas, "As the team's head brass": Does Thomas's use of blank verse seem to mimic the plowing of the field, especially given his emphasis upon "the turn" at the end of each furrow/line?

Stevens, "Sunday Morning" *CD-ROM Link

Eliot, "The Dry Salvages": Not in blank verse, but iambic pentameter surfaces in interesting ways from time to time; having students spot what they think are iambic-pentameter lines in section 5 (lines 184–215 in particular) is a good way to raise questions about the degree to which the metrical context of a line determines how we should scan it.

C. *Common Meter and Iambic Tetrameter/Trimeter (See "Versification")*

Employing quatrains in alternating lines of iambic tetrameter and iambic trimeter (usually with end-rhymes on the second and fourth lines), common meter is used so widely in hymns and ballads that it is also known as "ballad stanza" and "hymnal meter." It is probably the single form most easily recognized as a kind of verse by native speakers of English. A small selection of poems in common meter:

Anonymous, "Western Wind": This early song roughly approximates what later became a fixed form. You might ask your students to speculate on why these anonymous folk songs are rarely as regular in their use of the form as later lyrics written by individual authors who wrote common-meter verses perhaps to be sung, but first (or only) to be read. What role might increasing literacy have played? The printing press? The educated awareness of a long tradition of many poems in this form?

Anonymous, "Sir Patrick Spens": A classic example of a ballad in common meter. *CD-ROM Link

Philips, "To My Excellent Lucasia, on Our Friendship"

Massachusetts Bay Psalm Book, "Psalm 58"

Watts, "Our God, Our Help": A classic example of a hymn in common meter.

Blake, "The Divine Image"

Dickinson, #59 ("A little East of Jordan") and #254 ("'Hope' is the thing with feathers—"): Dickinson is simultaneously one of the most dedicated practitioners and most innovative experimentalists of common-meter. Virtually all of her poems can be construed as quatrains in approximate common meter form, but very few do not vary the standard pattern, usually in significant ways. An exercise: ask your students to identify the ways in which a Dickinson poem varies from common meter's expected pattern and to speculate on why she varies the pattern in the way she does. Does she suggest greater emphasis on a particular word or phrase that seems more unexpected for breaking with the established meter? Does she generate a sense of impromptu or naturalness? You might have them then regularize the poem, as you write their "corrected" version on the board. What is lost? Does this regularization change their ideas as to why she varied the pattern in the first place? Why not abandon the pattern entirely or experiment with another? What tensions do her verse forms suggest between restrictions and resistance that they might also find in the content of the poems?

Housman, "With Rue My Heart Is Laden": What subtle, almost unnoticeable variation in the standard common-meter pattern does this poem employ? This question might provide a good opportunity for students to practice traditional scanning. The first and third lines (the tetrameter lines) of each verse are "catalectic"—that is, they drop the final syllable of the meter to end on an unstressed syllable, using a trochaic word to end the line, i.e., "laden," "maiden," "leaping," "sleeping."

Cullen, "Incident"

In addition to the many well-known verses in the alternating iambic-tetrameter/trimeter lines of common meter, an enormous body of iambic poetry in English has been written wholly in tetrameter or trimeter lines, often in quatrains rhymed in the typical common-meter patterns of either *abcb* or *abab*, and it may be worthwhile to point out some of these variations on the common theme to your students. Although we use terms such as "blank verse" and "common meter" as though they referred to fixed entities, tracing the historical practice of verse forms means noting how even the most stable traditional patterns appear, on closer inspection, diversely interwoven with mutations and approximations. Difficult as it is to provide context when teaching from anthologies, common meter can be at least partly contextualized by comparing poems in the list immediately above with some of the tetrameter and trimeter selections below. What effects are lost when the alternating pattern of shorter and longer lines is swapped for consistent line length? Do the tetrameter quatrains seem more solid or the trimeter quatrains more terse than the quatrains in common meter? If your students assert that the differences are audible, ask them how they would characterize those differences and perhaps challenge them to distinguish differences due only to line length from differences due to all the other variables between the poems in question. Such a discussion can help to ground or initiate your students' own considerations of the ancient question as to how much and in what way traditional distinctions in versification actually correspond to meaningful differences between poems.

POEMS IN IAMBIC TETRAMETER

The four-beat line is associated with ballads, hymns, and songs. But it proves serviceable as well for epitaphs (**Jonson, Johnson**), religious poetry

(**Vaughan**), wittily erotic verse (**Donne, Herrick, Marvell**), and meditative verse, in which a voice contemplates the state of its own consciousness (**Milton, Bradstreet, Wordsworth**). In the modern era tetrameter has also been used to allude to the ballad or other traditions of popular verse (**Cummings, Eliot, Gunn**).

Anonymous, "There Is a Lady Sweet and Kind"
Wyatt, "My Lute Awake!"
Ralegh, "The Nymph's Reply to the Shepherd"
Campion, "When to Her Lute Corinna Sings"
Donne, "The Ecstasy"
Jonson, "On My First Daughter" and "Queen and Huntress"
Herrick, "The Vine" and "To Find God"
Carew, "A Song ('Ask me no more where Jove bestows')"
Milton, "L'Allegro" and "Il Penseroso": The tetrameters take over at line 11 in each poem; what has to be banished before this meter can be established?
Bradstreet, "Here Follows Some Verses upon the Burning of Our House July 10th, 1666"
Marvell, "Bermudas"
Vaughan, "The Retreat"
Blake, From *Poetical Sketches*, "Song" and from *Songs of Innocence*, "Introduction"
Wordsworth, "I Wandered Lonely As a Cloud"
Emerson, "Concord Hymn"
Tennyson, "Mariana": The first eight lines of each stanza are in tetrameter: what is the effect of the shift into ballad stanza (alternating tetrameter and trimeter lines) in the refrain?
Yeats, "Under Ben Bulben"
Frost, "Provide, Provide"
Eliot, "Sweeney Among the Nightingales"
Cummings, "my father moved through dooms of love"
Larkin, "An Arundel Tomb"
Momaday, "Two Figures"

POEMS IN IAMBIC TRIMETER

Askew, "The Ballad Which Anne Askewe Made and Sang When She Was in Newgate": This poem demonstrates that an exact ballad stanza was never a strict requirement. (Identifying itself as a ballad, the poem sticks with trimeter lines). Ballads, in fact, came in many verse forms; common meter, or ballad stanza, was simply the most widely used. Like many such traditional categories, the common-meter pattern of the ballad stanza was codified in retrospect, and the designation oversimplifies the historical diversity of ballad forms.

Ralegh, "The Lie"
Campion, "Now Winter Nights Enlarge"
MacNeice, "London Rain"
Roethke, "My Papa's Waltz"

D. Other Iambic Meters (See "Versification")

Although the vast majority of iambic poems in English are composed in three-, four-, or five-beat lines, occasionally one finds successful poems in shorter or longer line lengths. Monometer, however, is virtually unheard of in English, and poems with lines of more than six stressed syllables are mostly in free verse. Still, some productive class discussion may be generated by asking students why this has proven to be the case. After all, there is no law against heptameter, octameter, nonameter, or even decameter lines, and hexameter was actually the preferred length of classical epics and neoclassical French verse. Why are there so few metered poems in truly brief or truly lengthy lines in English? And if a poem consists of a hundred lines of blank verse, why not fifty lines of iambic decameter? Would it read any differently? Conversely, why are very short or long lines not at all uncommon in unmetered and free verse? (See, for instance, **W. C. Williams** and **Whitman,** respectively.) This last question may torpedo tentative answers to the first question that suggest that no poem could maintain audible rhythm or interest through very short or long lines.

POEMS IN IAMBIC HEXAMETER

Poems written wholly in iambic hexameter are rare (two notable examples, listed below, are by **P. Sidney** and **Dowson**); the hexameter line, or alexandrine, is more often used to lend solidity or stability at the end of a stanza written in a shorter measure. The closing alexandrine has varying functions in the Spenserian stanza of *The Faerie Queene*, and in its adaptations in English Romantic poetry, notably in **Shelley's** "Adonais" and **Keats's** "The Eve of St. Agnes." Spenser uses the hexameter close also for the resonant refrain of "Epithalamion." Partly in order to forge a link between his poetry and **Spenser's, Milton** ends the stanzas of "On the Morning of Christ's Nativity" with an alexandrine. Heroic couplets are sometimes varied by the occasional alexandrine, as in Dryden's "To the Memory of Mr. Oldham."

Queen Elizabeth I, "The doubt of future foes exiles my present joy": This poem is actually written in "poulter's measure," which alternated hexameter lines with heptameter lines and was named after the poulter's practice of counting fourteen eggs in the second dozen. Compare to P. Sidney's "What Length of Verse?", another poem in poulter's measure, but one using the long lines to parody the efforts of inferior sonneteers.

Spenser, From *The Faerie Queene*, Book 1 and "Epithalamion": Ask students to categorize the various ways Spenser uses the alexandrine to bring the stanza to a close. Does the alexandrine seem more a part of its stanza or a closed unit unto itself?

P. Sidney, From *Astrophel and Stella*, 1 ("Loving in truth, and fain in verse my love to show")

Milton, "On the Morning of Christ's Nativity"

Dryden, "To the Memory of Mr. Oldham"

Swift, "A Description of a City Shower": In this poem written in heroic couplets, what is the effect of the final hexameter line? How does it help to suggest the amount of assorted refuse that the flood collects?

Shelley, "Adonais"

Keats, "The Eve of St. Agnes"

Hardy, "The Convergence of the Twain"

E. *Meters Other Than Iambic (See "Versification")*

Since by far the major portion of poems in English, and hence in this anthology, are in some form of iambic meter, it is most sensible, we think, to teach as a unit poems written in trochaic, anapestic, and dactylic meters. Again, in subsequent discussion you might ask the students to speculate as to why these forms are so much rarer than iambics. Are they more difficult to compose? Do they sound strange or cacophonous?

TROCHAIC POEMS

Blake, "The Tyger": Blake's trochaic lines are irregular and often catalectic, ending on an odd-numbered, stressed syllable. Does this fact make the poem actually an iambic/trochaic hybrid? (In fact, the poem thereby gains a higher ratio of stressed to unstressed syllables than either strict iambic or trochaic meter would allow.) Do the opening trochees and the preponderance of stressed syllables give the lines a more propulsive force, and do they underscore the poem's composition as a series of rhetorical questions?

Graves, "Warning to Children"

ANAPESTIC POEMS

Anapests, because of their higher proportion of unstressed syllables, seem to move more quickly than iambs. Does this quickness make these poems more lively? What might be the drawbacks (such as an impression of frivolity or sing-song versifying)? Anapestic verse is perhaps the most common of the noniambic meters in English, and many iambic poems contain anapestic rhythms, especially where there are iambic/trochaic inversions or where secondary stresses are used to carry the iambic pattern. After introducing anapestics and anapestic poems, you might ask your students to search through examples of iambic poems for anapestic passages. Do these passages often mark shifts in tone or subject?

Montagu, "The Lover: A Ballad"
Swinburne, "A Forsaken Garden"
Hardy, "The Ruined Maid"

A DACTYLIC POEM

Hardy, "The Voice": "Dactyls are stately and classical," claims Coleridge's mnemonic for the meter. Ask your students if this seems to be the case here. Do the dactylic lines seem slower, in any event, than the lines of the anapestic poems above? Why?

F. Quantitative Meter (See "Versification")

Quantitative meter is the classical ancestor of the English accentual-syllabic meters discussed above and the source of most metrical terms (such as iambic, trochaic, etc.). However, classical quantitative metrics did not demand the alternation of stressed and unstressed syllables in a fixed pattern, but rather the alternation of "long" and "short" syllables. This method of measuring out lines by the relative lengths of their component syllables has not translated well into English; however, several poets, particularly during the Renaissance and Victorian periods, made heroic efforts to establish a poetics of quantification in English. An unusually successful example of an English poem written in an approximation of classical quantitative meter is **Campion's** "Rose-cheeked Laura." As a diverting classroom exercise, you could ask students to scan the poem on their own by simply deciding for themselves which syllables are longer or shorter. Ask them if they think there is any basis for counting longer or shorter syllables in English as we speak it now. And if not the quantitative meter, what then makes this poem still seem so artfully versified? It would probably not be wise, however, to introduce such an exercise in a class where students struggle when asked to identify syllables and stresses—tossing the red herring of syllabic "length" into their confusion would prove unhelpful at best.

G. *Scansion of Variable and Indeterminate Meters (See "Versification")*

Scansion can become a tedious exercise—can seem to abandon the reading of poetry in favor of applying to it an arcane arithmetic—when it becomes a matter simply of identifying what meter a line or group of lines is written in. It is worth emphasizing that lines don't have meters, poems do. Here is an exercise to heighten awareness of poetic rhythms and to demonstrate that it is often necessary to scan a line within the context of the entire poem in which it appears. The four-beat norm of ballads permits a varying number of unstressed syllables between strongly stressed syllables; this variation allows a four-beat line in an accentual meter to sound like a five-beat line in an accentual-syllabic meter. The line "For I crave one kiss of your clay-cold lips" in the early modern ballad "The Unquiet Grave" properly scans as a four-beat line in accentual or strong-stress meter: "For I crave one kiss of your clay-cold lips, / And that is all I seek." But if you insert this line into **Milton's** "Lycidas"—it fits rather nicely after line 14—it scans (technically, although it might not be read aloud as such) as iambic pentameter in an accentual-syllabic scheme, taking on the character of the lines preceding it: "He must not float upon his watery bier / Unwept, and welter to the parching wind, / Without the meed of some melodious tear. / For I crave one kiss of your clay-cold lips."

While it makes sense to introduce metrical feet by adducing words or phrases that illustrate that foot (e.g., "alone" is an iamb, "lonely" a trochee, "loneliness" a dactyl, and "all alone" an anapest), it prevents some confusion, in teaching scansion, to demonstrate that any of these words can be used quite comfortably to conform to any meter. The presence of, say, the word "everything" in a line does not mean that the line must be dactylic. Although "everything" is a dactyl, a stressed syllable followed by two unstressed ones, it can fit perfectly into an iambic meter, in which both its first syllable and its last syllable become stressed. We include a list of poems that incorporate the dactylic word "everything," in each of which it accommodates itself to another meter. Discussing in class the slight changes in emphasis and pronunciation that the word takes on in these examples is one way to train the ear for the rhythms of poetry. How does the word change in character in the anapests of "The Ruined Maid" and in the iambics of **Wordsworth** and **Frost**? In different iambic poems, how does the word "everything" take on altered emphases and rhythms from the shadings of its metrical context?

Wordsworth, "The World Is Too Much with Us": The winds that will be howling at all hours, / And are up-gathered now like sleeping flowers, / For this, for everything, we are out of tune . . .

Hardy, "The Ruined Maid": "O'Melia, my dear, this does everything crown! / Who could have supposed I should meet you in Town? . . ."

Yeats, "Under Ben Bulben": Where everything that meets the eye, Flowers and grass and cloudless sky . . .

When the word comes at the beginning of a line, as in the next example, how is its emphasis shaped by whether the preceding line is enjambed or end-stopped?

Frost, "The Wood-Pile": He thought that I was after him for a feather— / The white one in his tall; like one who takes / Everything said as personal to himself.

Of course, acknowledging the metrical flexibility of lines, phrases, and even single words means acknowledging that many whole poems are not only metrically variable but indeterminate. In the case of most metered poems, it is not the consistent application of meter throughout the poem that allows the poem to be identified as having such and such a meter. Rather, enough of the poem's lines display a prominently regular meter that we may safely claim the poem is in that meter, regardless of its variations. A great many poems considered to be composed in a particular meter, including our selections from **Blake's** *Songs of Innocence* and *Songs of Experience* and the majority of **Dickinson's** poems, seem to show more variation than repetition of the meter in question (mostly iambic tetrameter and trimeter in the cases of **Blake** and **Dickinson**). At what point do we concede that a poem is not in any one meter or even in an alternating pattern of two or more meters? There is no simple answer to this question. Have your students consider the poems below: are they metered? Or, what meters can the students identify within individual passages, and do these meters suggest a pattern for the whole poem or not? Instruct them to identify the stresses of individual words by the dictionary indications, but then to feel free to alter those patterns in accordance with what sounds natural to them when reading the lines aloud. This is a good opportunity for a workshop, either in groups or as a whole class. Poems like these let students see that meter is not as simple a matter as correct identification of a fixed entity. Where they disagree on a metrical pattern, ask them why. And finally, ask them to consider whether a poem that is not consistently built around a single meter or two alternating meters, but that shows stretches of various kinds of metrical regularity throughout its length, is indeed metered or unmetered. Encourage them to debate their responses to that question.

Leapor, "The Epistle of Deborah Dough"
Blake, "The Sick Rose"

Dickinson, #249 ("Wild Nights—Wild Nights!"), #303 ("The Soul selects her own Society—"), and #745 ("Renunciation—is a piercing Virtue—"): Which is a more significant source of repetition in these verses—meter or the apposition of parallel phrases?
Sissman, From "Dying: An Introduction," "IV. Path. Report"
Porter, "An Exequy"

1.3 Unmetered Verse (See "Versification")

There are other ways besides meter of creating regular patterns in verse. Although accentual-syllabic metrics based on terminology borrowed from the Graeco-Roman classical literatures have dominated English-language versifying since at least the sixteenth century, Old English poetry as well as some Middle English poetry was composed using a system of accentual verse and alliterative rhyme (see section 1.4D, "Alliteration"). Translations of the Bible into the English vernacular also influenced occasional approximations of Hebrew parallel verse, even when the rules of that form were unknown or poorly understood. And a few poets, particularly in this century, have attempted to build verses from syllable counts in preference to stress counts, a project nearly as difficult for English-language poets as the experiments in quantitative meter.

A. *Syllabics (See "Versification")*

Syllabic verse is the basis of Japanese poetry, but is rarely used in English, largely because syllable counts are not nearly as easy to hear as are stress patterns. Two twentieth-century poets who experimented extensively with syllabic forms, rhymed and unrhymed, were **Marianne Moore** and **Dylan Thomas. Thomas's** experiments were at least partly rooted in the ancient and complex syllabics of the Welsh, who were his ancestors. **Moore's** verse seems more idiosyncratic. Both poets, however, reveal one of the ways in which syllabics can be used effectively—through elaborate stanza forms with lines of sharply contrasting length.

Moore, "The Fish," "What Are Years?", "Nevertheless," and "The Mind Is an Enchanting Thing"
D. Thomas, "Fern Hill" *CD-ROM Link

B. *Accentual Verse (See "Versification")*

Alliterative accentual verse, which counts beats but disregards syllables, was the primary verse form of Old English poets and was rooted in oral tradition. Examples from this anthology demonstrate the range and flexibility of this verse form, including the elegiac "The Seafarer," the selection of Anglo-Saxon riddles, the epic of *Beowulf*, and Cædmon's "Hymn."

C. *Parallel Verse (See "Versification")*

Little poetry in English is written in regularized parallel syntax, although much poetry (and rhetorical prose, for that matter) employs stretches of parallel syntax of various kinds, sometimes for quite lengthy passages. Traditionally, the regular parallelism that undergirded the Hebrew poetics of the Bible was not seen as a verse form per se, and translations into English verse were generally into rhymed and metered stanzas. (See the various translations in this anthology of Psalm 58.) However, biblical parallelism seems to have been a primary influence on the loose and/or free verse of **Blake** and **Whitman,** to name but two, and a good contemporary example of a poem in parallel syntax can be found in **Palmer's** "Of this cloth doll which." If you bring to class a close translation in modern English of the Book of Psalms (Today's English Version or the New English Bible, for instance), you can ask your students to identify the pattern of parallel phrasing in one of the more familiar Psalms, such as 23 or 58, and compare with both the accentual-syllabic translations and Palmer's parallelism.

1.4 Rhyme (See "Versification")

One way to introduce students to rhyme is to adduce poems whose uses of rhyme are also implicit arguments about rhyme, such as **Dryden's** "A Song for St. Cecilia's Day" and **Keats's** "On the Sonnet." The question, for example, of whether rhyme is a freeing or imprisoning device of poetry is debated within some poems themselves. Thus, for **Dryden** rhyme represents or corresponds to a divine harmony, whereas for **Keats** rhyme is a cruel manacling of the muse. **Jonson** and **Milton** mock rhyme for its jangling effect on the ear and lack of a classical pedigree, although they both employ rhyme skillfully in many of their own poems. Rhyme sometimes sounds a dangerous lulling chime in **Poe** and **Tennyson. Lear** and **Blake** remind us, by the effect of their exact echoing, that we ordinarily expect rhyme words to sound a little different as well as the same. In defending rhyme against the charge of mere jingle, it is useful to ask students to look at particular pairs of rhymed words and to consider which ones are predictable or conventional (moon-soon, bowers-flowers) and which startling, in that they bring together words from utterly different realms of thought or discourse (saint-paint, gunnery-nunnery). Writers of light verse are fond of such unlikely pairings; writers of satirical verse (**Blake, Pope**) may sharpen their barbs by expressively shifting between conventional and startling rhymes. Another way to defend rhyme against jingle is to point out imperfect rhyme of various kinds.

Jonson, "A Fit of Rhyme Against Rhyme"

Herrick, "To the Virgins, to Make Much of Time": Almost a compendium of the *carpe diem* devices of seduction poetry (see section 17.1.A), its rhymes seeming as inevitable as its seductions, this is a good poem with which to teach the force of conventional rhyming. An exercise: before having students read this poem, give them the title and the first (or, where easier, second) word in each of the poem's rhymes; see if the class can come up with the completing rhymes. In a seduction poem, "marry" goes with "tarry" (as it also does, delightfully, in Lear's "The Owl and the Pussy-Cat"), just as surely as "sun" leads to some version of "run" (as it does at the end of Marvell's "To His Coy Mistress").

Dryden, "A Song for St. Cecilia's Day": Like most irregular odes, this one is good for teaching rhyme scheme, since the pattern differs in each stanza. How does the first stanza suggest that divine harmony is a kind of cosmic rhyme? Why is the first appearance of exact end rhyme delayed until line 7, with the words " 'Arise ye more than dead' "? (As the chaotic atoms become ordered, so does the rhyme scheme. The divine fiat is almost, here, "Let there be rhyme.")

Pope, "The Rape of the Lock" : You can dip in almost anywhere and find many instances of witty rhyming. Often Pope pairs rhymed words through the use of "zeugma": that is, the principle of pairing the serious and the trivial within a single line, often by making two unlike sounds the object of the same verb—"Or stain her honor or her new brocade" (Canto II, line 107). A similar effect is found within a pair of lines through rhyme, such as in "One speaks the glory of the British Queen, / And one describes a charming Indian screen" (Canto III, lines 13–14). What sorts of variety and surprise does Pope achieve by rarely rhyming two words that function as the same part of speech? For instance, in "Unnumbered throngs on every side are seen / Of bodies changed to various forms by Spleen" (Canto IV, lines 47–48), a verb ("seen") rhymes with a noun ("Spleen"), whereas the "Queen-screen" couplet (another rhyme on the *een* sound) pairs two incongruous nouns, and pairs them in a deflating or descending order. (For another comic rhyme on "Queen," see Canto IV, lines 57–58.)

Blake, "The Garden of Love" and "A Question Answered": How does the shift to markedly audible internal rhymes in the last two lines signal the unnatural binding of love by the priests? In "A Question Answered," how does rhyming the same line suggest a bitter refusal of witty antithesis? How does Blake undercut our expectations—established by the witty wars of the sexes in poets such as Pope and Swift—of having the second question answered with something like, "A pocket lined to buy them rich attire"? Compare the comic effect of Lear's use of this device of rhyming a line with the same line.

Byron, "So We'll Go No More A-Roving": How does this poem's grace derive in some measure from the utter conventionality of its rhymes (night-bright, soon-moon)?

Keats, "On the Sonnet": How does Keats's rhyme scheme loosen the muse's "garlands"? Compare to the rhyme schemes of other sonnets.

Tennyson, "The Lotos-Eaters": How does the opening of the poem suggest that the effect of rhyming a word with itself will not always be comical? How does the accumulation of lulling rhymes point toward the sailors' drug-deadened wish for changelessness?

Lear, "There Was an Old Man with a Beard" and "There Was an Old Man in a Tree": What is humorous about the flat rhyming of the same word at the end of the first and fourth lines? Have students make up a different last line with a different rhyming word and discuss the effects of this change.

Gilbert, "I Am the Very Model of a Modern Major-General": This patter song is an extravaganza of double, or "feminine," rhymes (see "Versification"). How does the heterogeneity of the words paired in these couplets figure the miscellaneous trivia a British commander had to know (instead of knowing how to command)?

D. Thomas, "In My Craft or Sullen Art": How many lines may intervene between two words before their rhyme is no longer detectable? Is "art" in line 1 too far removed from "heart" in line 11 for us to hear them as a rhyming pair? Do the intervening off-rhymes to "art" and "heart"—"night" and "arms"—preserve or confuse our memory of the initial rhyming word, "art," until its paired sound reaches our ear at the end of the stanza?

A. *Full, Perfect, and Partial Rhyme (See "Versification")*

It's worth pointing out to students that rhymes do not come only in the full, "cat-hat" or "heart-start," variety. It is possible to have a truly perfect rhyme pair of homonyms or even puns—"role-roll" or "lie" (deceive) and "lie" (recline)—known as "rime riche" (see "Versification"). By the same token, there is a broad spectrum of less-than-perfect rhymes, including partial or complete assonantal and consonantal rhymes, rhymes of unstressed syllables, and front rhymes (see section 1.4.D, "Alliteration"). All are rhymes and all are widely used throughout this anthology, often combined in the same text. Rhymes other than full rhymes go by many names—slant, near, off, imperfect, partial—but operate on the same principle: the intensified repetition, in regular or irregular patterns, of phonetic elements, whether they constitute consonants, vowels, parts of syllables, syllables, or entire words. A selection of poems using a variety of partial rhymes follows:

Dickinson, #465 ("I Heard a Fly buzz—when I died—"): Off-rhyme allows "Room" to rhyme with both "Storm" and "firm." Note that, as in a number of Dickinson's poems, the rhyme becomes perfect ("me-see"), in the last stanza (following the slant rhyme "be-Fly" in the penultimate stanza"): does this progression give the poem a surer finality? In #712 ("Because I could not stop for Death—"), what is the effect of the mixture of perfect and imperfect rhyme? Dickinson's first editors changed line 20 to "The Cornice but a mound": why did they think this would be an improvement? Is it? *CD-ROM Link
Crane, From *The Black Riders and Other Lines*
Frost, "Neither Out Far Nor In Deep": Do the full rhymes at the ends of the lines conceal any partial rhymes within the lines? (See section 1.4.B below.)
Sassoon, " 'They' "
Owen, "Strange Meeting": Is the unsettling effect of Owen's couplets in pararhyme (see "Versification") undercut by its predictability? Compare with other couplet poems with perfect rhyme.
Wilbur, "Advice to a Prophet"
Larkin, "For Sidney Bechet"
James Wright, "Speak"
Sexton, "The Truth the Dead Know"
Gunn, "A Map of the City"
T. Hughes, "The Thought-Fox"
Adcock, "The Ex-Queen Among the Astronomers"
Momaday, "Headwaters"
Harrison, "A Kumquat for John Keats"
Fenton, "In Paris with You"
Muldoon, "Milkweed and Monarch"

B. *End Rhyme and Rhyme Schemes (See "Versification")*

The varieties of rhyme schemes are more numerous even than the varieties of stanzas and lines that support them. A small selection indicating just how numerous these possibilities are might include:

Donne, "The Flea"
Gay, Songs from *The Beggar's Opera*
Poe, "The Raven"
Tennyson, "The Lady of Shalott"
Melville, "Monody"

Moore, "The Fish" and "The Mind Is an Enchanting Thing"
Millay, "The Buck in the Snow"
Toomer, "Reapers"
Auden, "Lullaby"
Bishop, "The Moose"
Hecht, "The Ghost in the Martini"
Merrill, "The Broken Home"
Snodgrass, From *Heart's Needle*
Jennings, "My Grandmother" and "One Flesh"
James Wright, "Speak"
Muldoon, "Milkweed and Monarch"
Leithauser, "In Minako Wada's House"
Schnackenberg, "Darwin in 1881"

C. *Internal Rhyme (See "Versification")*

What are the diverse effects of internal rhyming? Compare the celebratory or capering lilt it gives to the poems by **Nash** and **Lear** to the somber, elegaic note it strikes in the poems by **Coleridge** and **Tennyson.**

Nashe, "Spring, the Sweet Spring"
Blake, "The Garden of Love": What is the effect of the introduction of internal rhyme in the last two lines?
Coleridge, "The Rime of the Ancient Mariner": What is the effect of the occasional use of internal rhyme, as in lines 7, 22, 27, 31, and so on? Does the frequency of internal rhyme seem to respond to the tone or events of the poem?
Tennyson, "The Splendor Falls"
Lear, "The Owl and the Pussy-Cat"
Hopkins, "God's Grandeur"
Moss, "Tourists"
Merrill, From *The Book of Ephraim*
Murray, "Morse"
Heaney, "Digging"
Zarin, "Song"

D. *Alliteration (See "Versification")*

Alliteration was the dominant rhyming principle of early English verse, in which the general pattern was to alliterate two or three of the stressed syllables in a four-beat line. Regular alliteration structures the following poems:

Anonymous, "The Seafarer"
Anonymous, Riddles
Anonymous, *Beowulf*
Cædmon's "Hymn"
Anonymous, From *Pearl*
Langland, *Piers Plowman*

However, alliteration is rife throughout English-language poetry; the language alliterates frequently and almost effortlessly, and alliterative runs are much more easily generated than runs of full rhymes. Once your students have grasped the definition of alliteration, ask them to identify any samples that they can find in even a random thumb-through of their anthologies. Furthermore, some more-recent poets have tried to restore alliteration to a prominent place in modern versification, perhaps most notably **Hopkins** and **D. Thomas:**

Hopkins, "The Windhover," "Pied Beauty," "[As Kingfishers Catch Fire, Dragonflies Draw Flame]"
D. Thomas, "The Force That Through the Green Fuse Drives the Flower": Ask your students to compare the extravagant piling-on of alliteration in Thomas and Hopkins with the paced alliterative pairs of the anonymous Anglo-Saxon poets and Wilbur's poem below.
Wilbur, "Junk"

1.5 Free Verse

Which of these examples of free verse seem to have taken their cue from **Whitman,** allowing the line to spill its length along the page until the sentence it utters is finished? Which seem rather to be free verse for the typewriter, in the tradition of **Williams,** imposing a rough rule of an approximate number of characters per line? What range of effects does the ragged left-hand margin have? What principles may govern the line-breaks in free verse? Which poets tend to use line-ends to close a syntactic phrase, and which use line-ends to break or suspend a syntactic phrase? What different kinds of signals for reading the poem aloud are suggested in these diverse styles of free verse?

Whitman, "Song of Myself" *CD-ROM Link
Williams, "This Is Just to Say," "Poem," and "A Sort of a Song"
Lawrence, "Bavarian Gentians": The first line is iambic pentameter, but thereafter the lines expand. You might note that Lawrence's meter is free, but that his diction can be quite conventional or even

"high," as in the inversion of "arms Plutonic." (See section 6.3, "Diction.") *CD-ROM Link

Jeffers, "Birds and Fishes"

Eliot, "The Love Song of J. Alfred Prufrock" and "The Dry Salvages"

Warren, "Masts at Dawn"

Ammons, "Corsons Inlet"

O'Hara, "Why I Am Not a Painter"

Snyder, "Four Poems for Robin": The split lines of the first section may allude to the Old English form as imitated in Wilbur's "Junk." Why does the last poem fall into groupings of three, four, and five lines? Does this change indicate a growing, retrospective control and ordering, or a sense of loss and fragmentation?

Muldoon, "Gathering Mushrooms"

Lee, "Persimmons" *CD-ROM Link

CHAPTER 2

Stanzas

A poem written in stanzas comes to a series of temporary endings or completions, if only in the sense that an individual stanza comes to a close. How then does the poem sustain its energy? Sometimes what happens between stanzas can be as important as what happens within them. The list below singles out some notable uses of the stanza, to illustrate the variety of holds—some tight, some slack—that a stanza can have on the design and meaning of a poem. Some poets capitalize on the way stanzas may connect poems written in different eras; **Shelley,** for instance, borrows and revises established stanza forms such as the Spenserian stanza (in "Adonais") and terza rima (in "Ode to the West Wind"). Other poets, such as **Donne, Herbert, Swinburne,** and **Hardy,** are particularly inventive in devising new stanza forms for individual poems. In modern and contemporary verse there seems to be a new abundance of virtuosity and energy in inventing stanzas: could this fertility point to a way in which the increased freedom of modern and contemporary poetry leads to a desire for self-made restrictions? To describe a stanza fully, you must take into account the number of lines, their length, and the rhyme scheme; for which of the examples on the following list is the treatment of the left-hand margin also a defining feature of the stanza?

Donne, "Song ('Go and catch a falling star')" and "The Funeral"
Herrick, "An Ode for Him"

Herbert, "Easter Wings" and "The Flower"
Swinburne, "A Forsaken Garden"
Hardy, "The Convergence of the Twain": Do the stanzas "look like" the fatal iceberg? Are they diagrams of the operation of fate (two short, regular lines converge into a longer one)? For what other topics might this curious, bottom-heavy three-line stanza be appropriate?
Yeats, "The Stolen Child," "Byzantium," and "Long-Legged Fly"
Stevens, "Thirteen Ways of Looking at a Blackbird": For which poems on this list is each stanza a new "way of looking" at the poem's subject?
Eliot, "Preludes"
D. Thomas, "Fern Hill" *CD-ROM Link

2.1 Couplets and Heroic Couplets

A. *Couplets (See "Versification")*

Studying paired lines inevitably touches on a range of important issues in poetic form. What sorts of differences and affinities may prevail between the two words that rhyme in a couplet? How do the rhyming words invite us to look for symmetries, reflections, imbalances, logical coordinations, etc., between the paired lines as a whole? How do these questions become especially prominent in the heroic couplet ? Compare the closed couplets of Augustan satire to the more informal, conversational couplets of **Browning's** "My Last Duchess" and to the unrhymed couplets of Williams's "The Red Wheelbarrow." Couplets in iambic tetrameter—or octosyllabic couplets—are common, from **Milton's** "L'Allegro" and "Il Penseroso" to **Housman's** " 'Terence, This Is Stupid Stuff . . .' " and **Yeats's** "Under Ben Bulben." Varying effects of linking by rhyme two lines of markedly different length are illustrated in **Herrick's** "An Ode for Him" and the closing couplets of Donne's "The Canonization." An aphorism by Robert Frost might open up class discussion: "The couplet is the symbol of the metaphor."

Chaucer, "The Pardoner's Prologue and Tale" *CD-ROM Link
Anonymous, "The Three Ravens": What is the effect of the refrain's delaying of the second line's completion of the first line's sense and rhyme?
Askew, "The Ballad Which Anne Askewe Made and Sang When She Was in Newgate"
Queen Elizabeth I, "[The doubt of future foes exiles my present joy]"
Herrick, "Delight in Disorder," "An Ode for Him," and "To Find God"
Milton, "L'Allegro" and "Il Penseroso"
Marvell, "To His Coy Mistress"

Philips, "Epitaph"
Pope, "The Rape of the Lock"
Emerson, "Intellect"
R. Browning, "My Last Duchess"
Housman, " 'Terence, This Is Stupid Stuff . . .' "
Yeats, "Under Ben Bulben"
W. C. Williams, "The Red Wheelbarrow": See questions on Palmer's "Fifth Prose" below.
Jeffers, "Shine, Perishing Republic"
Owen, "Strange Meeting"
Bogan, "Juan's Song"
Birney, "Slug in Woods"
Moss, "Tourists"
Gunn, "A Map of the City"
Porter, "An Exequy"
Momaday, "Two Figures"
Palmer, "Fifth Prose": Ask your students how the visual emphasis on the couplet form in this poem (that otherwise would be considered free verse or prose poetry) differs from actually hearing rhymed couplets read aloud or in their heads. Are these really couplets? Does the term have any real meaning sans meter and rhyme? We seem to think the quatrain, at least, exists even when it's only a typographical creation—should we think so of all stanza forms, as long as we can count the lines? This is a good opportunity to point out how traditional forms cast historical shadows over free verse: it may be that the allusion to the idea of a couplet or other stanza form is significant, whether the purely visual stanza has any other unifying internal pattern or not.

B. Heroic Couplets (See "Versification")

The closed couplets of eighteenth-century poetry, with their witty antithesis, chiasmic twists of logic, balanced pairings, and droll anticlimaxes, are a good introduction to the rhetoric of poetry as well as to rhyme, lineation, and end-stopping. To get students to focus on the kind of labor that goes into crafting verse of this sort, assign twenty lines or so of any of these poems (say, the section on Belinda's dressing table from "The Rape of the Lock," Canto I, lines 121–40) and ask students to check off how many of these categories each set of rhymes belongs in; which rhymes pair different spellings for the same sound (unlocks-box), different parts of speech (arise-eyes), different numbers of syllables (unite-white), different etymologies or even different languages (rows–billet-doux), and—most important—different or opposed meanings (arms-charms). Students might then make some judgments about which poet pairs rhymes in the most varied and surprising ways.

Bradstreet, "Before the Birth of One of Her Children"
Cavendish, "An Apology for Writing So Much upon This Book"
Dryden, "Mac Flecknoe" and "To the Memory of Mr. Oldham"
Wilmot, "A Satire against Reason and Mankind"
Finch, "A Nocturnal Reverie"
Swift, "A Description of a City Shower"
Pope, "The Rape of the Lock" and "Epistle to Miss Blount"
Montagu, "The Lover: A Ballad"
Johnson, "The Vanity of Human Wishes"
Leapor, "Mira's Will"
Wheatley, "To S. M., a Young African Painter, on Seeing His Works"
Harrison, "A Kumquat for John Keats": Heroic couplets, dominant in the eighteenth century, are rarely seen in this century. How does Harrison loosen the meter? Does his use of this neoclassical stanza form seem in any way parodic? Why utilize a form associated with the Augustans in a poem addressed to a poet of the Romantic generation that effectively finished off the heroic couplet's reign as a major form in English?

2.2 Three-Line Stanzas: Tercets (See "Versification")

Three-line stanzas are not as numerous as couplets and quatrains. In which of these poems do tercets have the feeling of a riddle or a somewhat cryptic or incomplete statement? Is it our exposure to quatrains and couplets that tends to make some tercets feel either one line too long or one line too short? Poets who do use tercets tend to be fond of them. **Wallace Stevens** wrote most of his long poems in unrhymed tercets—indeed, the unrhymed tercet, with its ghostly allusion to the terza rima form of Dante's *Divine Comedy*, is employed in much of the meditative-epic poetry of the twentieth century. In addition to **Stevens, H. D.** and **Eliot** used this stanza form in their major late poetry.

Jonson, "A Fit of Rhyme Against Rhyme"
Herrick, "Upon Julia's Clothes": To demonstrate the different resources of and responses to tercets, quatrains, and couplets, rewrite this poem in two- and four-line units and discuss the effects of these revisions.
Shelley, "Ode to the West Wind": Does terza rima overcome the potentially incomplete feeling of a three-line stanza by its rhyming linkage (*aba bcb cdc*, and so on) of each stanza to the next? On terza rima, see "Versification.")
R. Browning, "A Toccata of Galuppi's"
Hardy, "The Convergence of the Twain"
Frost, "Provide, Provide"
Stevens, "Of Mere Being"

Williams, "Poem," "The Yachts," and "Asphodel, That Greeny Flower": How do Williams's staggered tercets in "Asphodel, That Greeny Flower" both open the form to a kind of continuous scrolling and maintain some unity within each three-line group?
H. D., From "The Walls Do Not Fall"
Jacobsen, "Hourglass"
Swenson, "Goodbye, Goldeneye"
Larkin, "For Sidney Bechet" and "Sad Steps"
Plath, "Morning Song," "Ariel," and "Lady Lazarus"
Strand, From *Dark Harbor*, XVI
Zarin, "The Ant Hill"

2.3 Four-Line Stanzas: Quatrains (See "Versification")

Quatrains are the most common stanza form in English poetry. More than any other form they seem to suggest self-containment and closure, especially when they consist of end-rhymed lines of equal length. And yet long poems in quatrains are common, and the lyric narratives of ballad stanzas prove that quatrains can carry a story well. How does a series of quatrains avoid becoming simply a collection of insular units? Enjambment, refrain, and overlapping rhyme scheme are a few of the strategies that poets employ to bridge quatrains.

The selection below represents a small fraction of the poems in quatrains in this anthology. The section on "Common Meter and Iambic Tetrameter/Trimeter" (1.2.C) also contains several examples of poems in quatrains.

Behn, "Song ('Love Armed')"
Montagu, "A Receipt to Cure the Vapors"
Elliot, "The Flowers of the Forest"
Barbauld, "The Rights of Woman" *CD-ROM Link
Gray, "Elegy Written in a Country Churchyard"
FitzGerald, "The Rubáiyát of Omar Khayyám of Naishápúr"
Brontë, "No Coward Soul is Mine": What is the effect of the alternation of trimeter and pentameter lines? How would the effect be different if the stanza were organized 5-3-5-3 instead of 3-5-3-5? In most quatrains of alternating longer and shorter lines, the shorter lines are lines 2 and 4, not 1 and 3 (for example, popular ballads, Wordsworth's, "A Slumber Did My Spirit Seal"). This exception to the norm invites speculation on why shorter lines tend to follow longer ones and not the other way around.
Clough, "[Say not the struggle nought availeth]"
Frost, "Neither Out Far Nor In Deep"
Pound, "Hugh Selwyn Mauberley": Pound and Eliot decided in the

1910s to move away from free verse and "general floppiness" (as Pound put it) back to tight, rhymed tetrameter quatrains. How do these poems stretch the capacity of this form by stuffing it with polysyllabic words, fragments from other texts, and languages other than English? Conversely, how does the form seem to force compression and elision on its contents?

Eliot, "Sweeney Among the Nightingales": See above questions.

Cummings, "somewhere I have never travelled, gladly beyond," "anyone lived in a pretty how town," and "my father moved through dooms of love"

Cullen, "Incident"

Warren, "Bearded Oaks"

Hope, "Australia"

Hayden, "Night, Death, Mississippi"

Wilbur, "Piazza di Spagna, Early Morning"

Hecht, "The Ghost in the Martini"

Ormond, "Cathedral Builders"

Snodgrass, From *Heart's Needle*, 10

Sexton, "The Truth the Dead Know"

Gunn, "The Missing"

MacPherson, "A Lost Soul"

Adcock, "The Ex-Queen Among the Astronomers"

Momaday, "The Gift"

Murray, "Noonday Axeman"

Duffy, "Warming Her Pearls"

2.4 Longer Stanzas

Generally, the longer the stanza form, the rarer the usage. However, a great many poems in this anthology feature regular stanzas of five to ten lines or more. You might ask your students whether the longer stanzas seem to break into smaller sub-stanza units within themselves. An exercise: copy out a poem in longer stanzas as a single unit, then encourage your students to relineate the text, providing stanza breaks at the points where they themselves feel breaks belong. Then discuss the reasons for their choices and consider possible reasons for the poet's choice of stanza form. This exercise might also dovetail nicely with discussion of poems' development and internal structures (see section 3.3, "Transitions and Middles").

A. *Cinquaines, Sestets, and Septets (See "Versification")*

Wyatt, "The Lover Showeth How He Is Forsaken of Such as He Sometime Enjoyed" ("They Flee from Me"): This poem is an example of the elaborate Renaissance stanza form "rhyme royal" (see "Versification"). *CD-ROM Link

Bradstreet, "The Prologue"
Gay, Songs from *The Beggar's Opera*, "Air IV"
Melville, "Monody"
Moore, "The Fish" and "The Mind Is an Enchanting Thing"
Bishop, "The Moose"
Larkin, "An Arundel Tomb"
Snodgrass, From *Heart's Needle*, 2, 3, 7
Jennings, "My Grandmother" and "One Flesh"
Komunyakaa, "Banking Potatoes"
Leithauser, "In Minako Wada's House"

B. *Ottava Rima and Other Eight-Line Stanzas (See "Versification")*

Mary Sidney, "Psalm 58: *Si Vere Utique*"

Byron, From *Don Juan*: This entire satirical epic was composed in ottava rima and contains some of the wittiest, most bravura rhyming in the history of the English language.

Yeats, "Sailing to Byzantium" and "Among School Children": Both of these poems were written in ottava rima. Ask students to compare the poems: does the stanza form operate any differently between them? Does it have any effect on tone? Organization? How do these long stanzas seem to mark discrete smaller poems within the larger sequence?

Larkin, "MCMXIV"

C. *Spenserian and Other Nine-Line Stanzas (See "Versification")*

Spenser, *The Faerie Queene*, Book 1

Keats, "The Eve of St. Agnes": One of the curiosities of the Spenserian stanza is that it is often used in poems that look backward at the medieval period. Spenser's own language was artificially archaic, and both Keats and Tennyson use the form for poems with anachronistic medieval themes. Does anything about the form itself strike your students as especially suggestive of great antiquity?

Shelley, "Adonais": If your students have read "The Eve of St. Agnes," you might ask them why Shelley might choose the stanza form used in that poem for his elegiacal tribute to Keats.

Tennyson, "The Lady of Shalott" and "The Lotos-Eaters": In the latter poem, the Spenserian stanza is used through line 45. What diverse associations has the form accumulated by the time Tennyson comes to use it? Does Tennyson's model seem to be Spenser himself, the

Romantic poets (such as Keats and Shelley) who inherited the Spenserian stanza, or some amalgam of the two?

Auden, "Lullaby"

D. Stanzas of Ten Lines or More

Anonymous, From *Pearl*
Behn, "The Disappointment"
Finch, "Adam Posed"
Donald Hall, From "The One Day," "Prophecy"

2.5 Variable and Free Stanza Patterns (See "Versification")

Stanzas, of course, are not confined to recurring patterns. During the eighteenth century, a mistaken understanding of the Pindaric ode led to the composition of many "great odes" in elaborately varied stanzas. Later, **Whitman** composed his rolling free-verse lines in long, uneven stanzas, and the twentieth century has seen more poetry in irregular than in regular stanza form.

Finch, "The Spleen"
Barbauld, "Life"
Wordsworth, "Ode: Intimations of Immortality"
Whitman, "Song of Myself" *CD-ROM Link
Auden, "In Memory of W. B. Yeats" *CD-ROM Link
Schnackenberg, "Darwin in 1881"
Erdrich, "I Was Sleeping Where the Black Oaks Move"
Lee, "Persimmons" *CD-ROM Link

CHAPTER 3

Frames and Development

Because poems appear to students already fixed and timeless, teaching the ways in which poems are framed and developed can easily turn into dusty "take-my-word-for-it" lectures by the instructor and numbing line-by-line readings by the students, showing no sense of the overall structure or unexpected turns of the texts they explicate. One way to shake things up a little is to present students with pieces of poems and then challenge them to supply the following or previous lines/stanzas. Students can compare their predictions to each other's and to the revealed poem; discussion can center around why the poet might have made the choices that they did not—or around why a student who closely approximated the actual poem came up with that approximation and what that might tell us about the poet's thinking during composition. Students should be encouraged to have and express their own opinions as to which solutions are better, even if that occasionally means they prefer one of their own to the "classic." And, to combine this lesson with lessons in versification, you might require that the students draft their own lines in the form of the original's. Several of these exercises are suggested below; you may prefer to have students work singly or in small groups—whichever seems more productive and less intimidating to your class will probably work best. An example: ask students to construct a poem that follows from the first four words of **W. C. Williams's** "The Red Wheelbarrow," with the stricture that they must maintain the exact form of distiches made up of a three- or four-syllable top line followed by a two-syllable, one-word (or word-fragment) bottom line, the whole thing adding up to only one sentence. Because no rhyme or meter is involved and there are no restrictions on subject matter, this task is not as difficult as it may at first sound. It also leads to interesting discussions of how important those first four abstract words are to the significance of this tiny, cryptic, concrete, imagist poem. (See section also 3.2.A, "First Lines".)

3.1 Titles

The naming of poems is as rich and varied as other poetic devices. Often a fruitful technique in teaching any poem can be inventing, or asking the class to invent, one or two alternate titles for the poem and discussing the range of different expectations and interpretations these titles suggest. Or use a specific, occasion-marking title, such as **Keats's** "On Sitting Down to Read *King Lear* Once Again," as an alternative title for a different poem, such as **Donne's** "The Sun Rising" or **Herbert's** "Artillery." What expectations are established—and which ones denied—when a title includes the genre the poem belongs to, as in **Keats's** "Ode to a Nightingale"? What features of a poem may a title be unable to, or fail to, take into account? Which poems have titles that seem to make sense right from the first line? Which poems seem rather to have to earn their titles? Which titles seem to have a strong interpretive force, urging us to respond to the poem in a way dictated by the title? Which titles seem less directive to the reader? The titles of some poems, of course, such as popular ballads, become attached to poems over time for reasons of convenience. Some poems, by design or convenience, are simply labeled by their opening lines: for which poems is such a title a useful aid to interpretation, and for which is it merely a way to differentiate one poem from another? In which poems whose title is the first line does that first line take on a deeper or emblematic resonance, so that it seems to oversee or name the whole poem rather than just to initiate it? How do conventions of titling poems change over history? What sorts of titles come in and out of vogue? We have suggested some groupings of poems that share similar titles, or that seem to be titled according to similar principles.

A. *Titles that Allude or Address*

POEMS WITH ALLUSIVE TITLES

What is the effect of a title that alludes to another poem, sometimes in another language, or to another source? How much of the context of the poem alluded to in the title does the poem draw upon, or ask us to be familiar with?

Owen, "Dulce Et Decorum Est"
Larkin, "MCMXIV"
Hecht, " 'More Light! More Light!' "
Schnackenberg, "Darwin in 1881"

Poems with Titles of Address

Often a title directs the poem to a specific hearer, reader, or audience. Another poem so addressed might not indicate it so plainly in its title; nor does such a title necessarily exclude other audiences. A topic for a student paper toward the end of an introductory course might be a discussion of all the things "to" can mean in such a title. What does it mean to write a poem "to" someone or something? How may writing a poem *to* someone differ from writing a poem *for* someone? What is our role as audience to poems written for a specific someone? Does such a title turn all other readers than the one addressed into eavesdroppers? Can reading such a poem be like reading a letter that is not addressed to us? Or do we necessarily stand in for the person or object such a poem claims to be addressing?

Chaucer, "Complaint to His Purse"
Skelton, "To Mistress Margaret Hussey"
Drayton, "To the Reader of These Sonnets"
Herrick, "To the Virgins, To Make Much of Time"
Carew, "Song. To My Inconstant Mistress"
Bradstreet, "The Author to Her Book"
Marvell, "To His Coy Mistress"
Philips, "To My Excellent Lucasia, on Our Friendship"
Burns, "To a Mouse"
Keats, "Ode to a Nightingale"
Whitman, "To a Locomotive in Winter"
Douglas, "Vergissmeinnicht"
Kinnell, "The Correspondence School Instructor Says Goodbye to His Poetry Students"

B. *Titles of Occasion*

What is the effect of the peculiar specificity of a title that names a specific occasion, that places the poet in a certain place and time either at the writing of the poem or at its conception? How may such a title bring the reader's attention, from the outset, to the act of composing the poem—or simply to the fact that the poem was composed at a certain time in response to a certain moment or event? How is our reading of the poem influenced by this initial turn of our attention to the act of writing the poem? How does the title suggest links to other genres, such as journals, diaries, and letters?

Donne, "Good Friday, 1613. Riding Westward"
Bradstreet, "Here Follows Some Verses upon the Burning of Our House July 10th, 1666"
Wheatley, "To S. M., a Young African Painter, on Seeing His Works"
Wordsworth, "Composed upon Westminster Bridge, September 3, 1802"
Byron, "Written After Swimming from Sestos to Abydos"
Keats, "On Sitting Down to Read *King Lear* Once Again"
D. Thomas, "A Refusal to Mourn the Death, by Fire, of a Child in London"

C. Titles that Suggest the Poem's Purpose

Wyatt, "The Lover Showeth How He Is Forsaken of Such as He Sometime Enjoyed" ("They Flee from Me") *CD-ROM Link
Donne, "A Valediction Forbidding Mourning" *CD-ROM Link
Jonson, "Inviting a Friend to Supper"
Hope, "Inscription for a War"
Jacobsen, "Hourglass"
James Wright, "Speak"
Wilner, "Reading the Bible Backwards"
Muldoon, "Gathering Mushrooms"

D. The Grammar of Titles

Titles that are full declarative sentences: why are these so rare? Why are poem (and other) titles so rarely statements, but most often fragments of various sorts, incomplete phrases needing to be filled out by the poem? Why are the names of poems more often names of things or people than statements about what they do ("Badger," "The Rhodora," "The Prisoner"; "Mr. Flood's Party," not "Mr. Flood Gives a Party")? When poem titles include verbs, why are they often in some form of the progressive ("Inviting a Friend to Supper," "Crossing the Bar," "Crossing Brooklyn Ferry," "Sailing to Byzantium," "Boy Breaking Glass," "Naming of Parts," "Waking from Sleep," "Living in Sin")?

Sir Philip Sidney, "What Length of Verse?"
R. Browning, "The Bishop Orders His Tomb at St. Praxed's Church"
L. Hughes, "The Negro Speaks of Rivers"
Kinnell, "The Correspondence School Instructor Says Goodbye to His Poetry Students"
Raine, "A Martian Sends a Postcard Home"

E. *Titles Suggesting Other Kinds of Art*

Titles that seem to belong to, or are borrowed from, some mode of discourse other than poems become more common in this century. What changes in twentieth-century poetry does this tendency suggest? What is the effect of giving to a poem the sort of title usually thought more appropriate to a painting, a musical composition, or a how-to manual?

Stevens, "Thirteen Ways of Looking at a Blackbird"
Pound, "Portrait d'une Femme"
Eliot, From *Four Quartets*

F. *Epigraphs*

A number of nineteenth-century poems and a larger number of twentieth-century poems that do not explicitly cite a source within the poem itself allude to some earlier text through the use of an epigraph or motto—a brief quotation placed at the head of the poem. What diverse relations may obtain between poem and epigraph? Does the poem illustrate the epigraph, contemplate it, revise it, or simply use it as an inviting or intriguing introduction into the poem? When may the epigraph function as an alternative title?

Barbauld, "Life"
Wordsworth, "Ode: Intimations of Immortality": Why is it appropriate for this poem to have as an epigraph a passage from an earlier poem by Wordsworth himself?
Coleridge, "The Rime of the Ancient Mariner": The epigraph to "Dejection: An Ode" is from the anonymous ballad "Sir Patrick Spens" (*CD-ROM Link), in a version somewhat different from the one in the anthology.
Shelley, "Adonais"
Tennyson, "Mariana"
Pound, "The Garden," "Hugh Selwyn Mauberley"
Eliot, "The Love Song of J. Alfred Prufrock," "Sweeney Among the Nightingales," and *The Waste Land*
Hope, "Inscription for a War"
Reed, "Lessons of the War": What is the effect of the change Reed makes in the lines from Horace?
R. Lowell, "For the Union Dead": What is the effect of heading a poem with an inscription from a monument?
Clampitt, "Beethoven, Opus 111"
Douglas, "Aristocrats"
Wilbur, "Junk"

Snodgrass, From *Heart's Needle*
Hill, "An Apology for the Revival of Christian Architecture in England"
Mahon, "A Disused Shed in Co. Wexford"

3.2 Opening Moves

Like the first brushstroke on a bare canvas, delineating what was formerly bare space, the first line of a poem is irrevocable, a signing of a contract. A poem may begin with the decisive opening wedge of an exclamation, or with an offhand conversational remark, or with a grand pronouncement. A poet may begin in the mode of a storyteller, giving the source of what he or she is about to relate, or else may begin by shocking the reader into attention. The poem's first inroad on silence may be a sigh or an outcry ("Ah, Ben!"; "Out upon it!"; "Gr-r-r—there go, my heart's abhorrence!"; "Shut, shut the door, good John!"); a reprimand ("Ay, beshrew you! by my fay"; "For God's sake hold your tongue, and let me love"; "Get up! get up for shame!"; "Hence vain deluding Joys"); a question—sometimes demanding an answer and sometimes not ("Why does your brand sae drap wi' bluid?"; "How do I love thee?")—or a confession ("I, too, dislike it"; "I want a hero"). A poem may begin with a generalization or an adage that may not seem to require any proof or amplification ("All human things are subject to decay"; "Something there is that doesn't love a wall"), or with an extravagant claim or boast that seems to require the entire poem's effort to make good on ("I heard a Fly buzz—when I died—"; "How like an angel came I down!"). Or a poem can start as if it were already underway before we've started reading it ("And then went down to the ship"). A first line can be packed, stacking the deck, presenting a formed opinion ("An old, mad, blind, despised, and dying king"; "Terence, this is stupid stuff"), or it may be hanging in midair, a subordinate clause promising a complex syntactic chain before the thought launched in the first line is completed ("Having been tenant long to a rich lord"; "Of man's first disobedience, and the fruit"; "since feeling is first"). A poem may begin with a report on the time and weather ("The sea is calm tonight"; "There are no stars to-night"; "I am driving; it is dusk"; "It is 12:20 in New York a Friday"; "Late summer, and at midnight"; "St. Agnes' Eve—Ah, bitter chill it was!"). Or it may set up the reader's expectations with a burst of exotic names ("In Xanadu did Kubla Khan") or familiar ones ("Just off the highway to Rochester, Minnesota").

One thing this list will suggest is that the index in the anthology is a useful teaching tool. Assigning as a group all the poems that begin "Let . . . " is a good way to examine the range of ways a poem can invite, enjoin, seduce, and suggest. Similarly, a selection from the large group of poems that begin "I . . . " can suggest interesting ways to introduce questions of poetic persona and voice. Or reading as a group all the poems that begin with some version of an announcement of the prevailing weather (a surprisingly large group, and not just from the Romantic era, as one might expect) is one way to introduce the question of setting. Asking how a poem fulfills, alters, or breaks the promises (of tone, language, meter, subject) that its first line appears to make is something we do implicitly all the time when we invoke such categories as poetic unity or coherence. Some poets are more skilled at memorable openings than others: **Dickinson, Arnold,** and **Lawrence** are three very different poets who often begin their poems in especially striking ways. Asking a class what qualities an effective first line should have is a good way of getting them to think about broader questions concerning what kinds of things they believe poems are or should be about and how they think poems should talk about those things. Pick other lines out of poems; would they be suitable openings? What could we reasonably expect a poem that began with one of these lines to go on to say? A related and important idea that can emerge from such questions is that we come to poems with expectations based on our experience of what kinds of things poems tend to say, and that poets depend on such readerly expectations, even if they set out to subvert them.

A. *First Lines*

As an exercise, give students a sampling of first lines and ask them to predict what each poem is about, what its mood might be, and/or what comes next. Another exercise: place several of the most famous opening lines on the board (e.g., **Chaucer's, E. B. Browning's**) and ask students if they seem familiar. As a follow-up, compare those lines to two or three famous opening lines from plays and/or novels (e.g., Dickens's *A Tale of Two Cities*).

Anonymous, "The Seafarer"

Chaucer, "The General Prologue": The first few lines of *The Canterbury Tales* are perhaps the most famous opening lines of any poem in English. Compare them with the opening of Eliot's *The Waste Land*, three lines that allude to Chaucer's lines and are nearly as famous—and ask students how the same time of year can be productive of such opposite introductory atmospherics. (See section also 16.6.A, "Spring and Summer.") How do opening lines set the scene for the whole poem?

Queen Elizabeth I, "[Ah silly pugg wert thou so sore afraid]": Here is an unusual example of intimate address from a monarch to a favorite courtier. Ask your students to characterize the relationship of the speaker and the addressee from just this opening line.

Marlowe, "The Passionate Shepherd to His Love": How is the shepherd's invitation, "Come live with me and be my love," also in some sense an invitation to the reader? An exercise: have students try to find any other poems that begin with invitations. *CD-ROM Link

Shakespeare, Sonnet 18 ("Shall I compare thee to a summer's day?"): Many poems end with questions; many also begin with them. How does a question set the reader's expectations for a poem? Compare the opening of this sonnet to the opening question of Blake's "The Tyger" and perhaps the closing question of Yeats's "Among School Children"—if a closing question hangs in the air, its answer forever indeterminate, does an opening question serve as notice that the rest of the poem is its answer?

Donne, "Song ('Go and catch a falling star')": How does opening a poem with an imperative affect the reader's expectation of the rest of the poem?

Marvell, "To His Coy Mistress"

Blake, "The Tyger"

Wordsworth, *The Prelude*, Book I ("Fair seedtime had my soul, and I grew up"): How does the burden of an opening line to such a long, autobiographical poem differ from the task of opening a song lyric, a sonnet, or even an epigram?

E. B. Browning, Sonnets from the Portugese, 43 ("How do I love thee? Let me count the ways")

Dickinson, #465 ("I heard a Fly buzz—when I died—"): Here the issue is not just the opening line but the two halves of the opening line, with the interpolated dash suggesting almost the careful pause preceding a punch line, the first half of the line consisting of a banal observation, the second of a voice from beyond the grave.

Eliot, "The Love Song of J. Alfred Prufrock" and *The Waste Land*

Bishop, "The Fish"

Ginsberg, "Howl," Part I

Glück, "Gretel in Darkness"

Kenney, "Apples on Champlain"

Daniel Hall, "Mangosteens"

Soto, "Not Knowing": How do the first two words, "By then," set the scene for the poem by implying a long prelude to its events?

Schnackenberg, "Darwin in 1881"

Zarin, "The Ant Hill"

B. *Initial Situations*

Even a brief, nonnarrative lyric can conjure up transformations, changes of scene or of heart, magical epiphanies, and so forth. In such a case, the poem's success in establishing the initial scene prior to the change of perspective is crucial. Here follows a short list of poems that create the fiction of an initial situation in order to effect its transformation.

Shakespeare, Sonnet 73 ("That time of year thou mayst in me behold")
Donne, "The Sun Rising": This poem is an example of a "morning song," also known as an "alba" or "aubade," in which a lover complains of the arrival of dawn, apparently after a night of passionate but secret love. How does Donne turn his complaint with the initial situation into an extravagant boast? Compare to Kenney's recent example of the genre, "Aubade," below.
Swift, "The Lady's Dressing Room"
Wordsworth, "Lines Composed a Few Miles Above Tintern Abbey"
Tennyson, "Mariana"
R. Browning, "My Last Duchess"
Dickinson, #754 ("My Life had stood—a Loaded Gun")
Hopkins, "[No Worst, There Is None. Pitched Past Pitch of Grief]"
Robinson, "Richard Cory"
Frost, "Stopping by Woods on a Snowy Evening"
Moore, "The Steeple-Jack"
L. Hughes, "Theme for English B"
Jacobsen, "Hourglass"
Bishop, "The Moose"
O'Hara, "The Day Lady Died": Why is it important for this poem that we first feel the utter ordinariness of the day on which the speaker learns of Billie Holiday's death?
Momaday, "Headwaters"
Kenney, "Aubade"

3.3 Transitions and Middles

We don't mean to suggest by this section and the ones preceding and following it that poems are tripartite structures, but simply that it can be instructive to think of some poems as mapping for themselves an itinerary that enables them to get from the opening to the close. This journey may not be explicitly narrative, but some poems may be thought of as telling a story of their own unfolding. An exercise may help to convince beginning students that they already read poetry with some assumptions about what a poem's progress looks like: choose a short poem, give students the first and last parts (perhaps poems in stanzas would work best), and ask them to write an approximation of what seems most likely to come between the these parts. For which poems are students able most accurately to predict or invent the middles? For which poems is the route from beginning to end most circuitous or surprising?

A. *Narrative Development*

Students may tend to think of poems as moments of emotion or contemplation, but it is important to remind them that poems can also tell stories. Perhaps all poems do, even very short ones; what kind of story might we invent as background for "Western Wind," for example? Or maybe it is more accurate to say that all poems have a plot, or at least follow some progression or narrative of their own unfolding. Most of the early modern ballads tell stories, often in highly abbreviated ways; we've listed only a few here that seem especially useful for helping students reflect on how poems do so. Story poems can be long, detailed yarns ("The Rime of the Ancient Mariner") or blunt, tight-lipped recountings of a life ("The Death of the Ball Turret Gunner"). So many poems could be said to give an account of events or unfold a tale of some kind that this list attempts merely to suggest the range possible in narrative poems.

Anonymous, "Sir Patrick Spens" (*CD-ROM Link) and "Mary Hamilton"

Herbert, "The Pulley": This poem is like a "just-so story," telling how something came about, giving the story that resulted in a present condition—in this case, why human beings are always restless and unsatisfied, no matter what blessings they enjoy.

Pope, "The Rape of the Lock"

Blake, "I Askéd a Thief"

Coleridge, "The Rime of the Ancient Mariner"

Keats, "The Eve of St. Agnes"

R. Browning, "My Last Duchess"

Arnold, "The Scholar-Gypsy": You might treat this poem as a ghost story.

Dickinson, #712 ("Because I could not stop for Death—") *CD-ROM Link

Housman, "Is My Team Plowing"

Yeats, "Lapis Lazuli": What kind of story does the speaker find in or fabricate about the carved figures? Compare to the kinds of little narratives told about the scenes on the urn in Keats's "Ode on a Grecian Urn."

Frost, "The Road Not Taken": This is perhaps a good introductory poem for this group, as it invites discussion of the ways we tell stories about our lives in order to make sense of them. That is, if the two roads were about the same, how could it have made all the difference which one the speaker chose? Why is it more comforting to think of our lives as irrevocably shaped by proceeding through a series of crucial forks in the road, than as simply one long continuous journey of random routes? Compare with the picture Coleridge's Ancient Mariner gives of the decisions or accidents that shaped the journey of his life.

Jarrell, "The Death of the Ball Turret Gunner": How does Jarrell tell a whole life in five lines? What sort of a life is it that can be told so tersely? Exercise: rewrite "The Rime of the Ancient Mariner," or any of the poems in this list, in five lines or so, using Jarrell's poem as a model.

O'Hara, "The Day Lady Died"

B. *Nonnarrative Development*

Ask your students to try to map the twists and turns of a meditative/expressive poem that does not seem to have any significant narrative component. What changes occur between the opening and closing lines? An exercise: bring in photocopied parts of a few essentially nonnarrative poems and ask students to suggest what might come before or come next (perhaps in small group workshops). Compare their various suggestions to each other and then to the actual progress of the poem. Discuss the surprises and the nonsurprises and consider the possible reasons why the poems develop as they do.

Cædmon's "Hymn"

Anonymous, "The Seafarer"

Anonymous, "Now Go'th Sun Under Wood": How does this lyric fold two narratives, one ordinary (the end of a day) and one extraordinary (the Crucifixion), into one short cry of grief?

Wyatt, "The Lover Showeth How He Is Forsaken of Such as He Sometime Enjoyed" ("They Flee from Me") *CD-ROM Link

Spenser, *Amoretti*: Compare with Wroth's "Crowne of Sonnets" below. Is the development of themes within individual poems more or less significant than the development of the sonnet sequence itself? (See also section 4.8.A, "Sonnet Sequences.")

Donne, Holy Sonnet 10 ("Death, be not proud, though some have called thee"): How is Donne's argument organized? How is this poem reminiscent of a rhetorical essay?

Wroth, from "A Crowne of Sonnets Dedicated to Love"

Waller, "Song": The lover's commissions to the rose work out the resemblances between the rose and the coy mistress; how does the middle stanza then stretch the bow taut to release the shaft of "Then die!" in the last stanza? Compare to the progression of argument in other seduction poems.

Gray, "Elegy Written in a Country Churchyard": How does this poem use the device of a thoughtful walk in the country to structure its succeeding images and reflections?

Poe, "The Raven": This poem is often seen as a narrative, and yet its only event is the arrival of the Raven, after which all is nightmarish repetition. Repetitiveness is its own strategy of development: how does it serve to reinforce the Raven's message here? (See also section 3.6, "Refrains.")

Keats, "To Autumn"

Hayden, "Night, Death, Mississippi"

Wilner, "Reading the Bible Backwards"

Graham, "Opulence"

Schnackenberg, "Darwin in 1881"

Zarin, "The Ant Hill"

C. *Turning Points*

Virtually all poems, narrative or nonnarrative, epic or lyric, contain turning points in the progress of the text. Epigrams, though generally only two to four lines long, are characterized, much like stand-up comedy, by set-ups for ironic or satiric twists. Even the anonymous medieval quatrain "Western Wind" turns from the querulous atmospherics of its first two lines ("Western wind, when will thou blow, / The small rain down can rain?") to the explosive sigh of the last two lines ("Christ, if my love were in my arms / And I in my bed again!"). Calling your students' attention to this nearly essential feature of poetry, you might first find turns in a few small poems, then in a few longer but nonnarrative texts, and then discuss a complex narrative poem, perhaps an excerpt from *Beowulf* or *The Canterbury Tales* or *The Faerie Queene*. Are turning points in poems the same thing as plot events? How can a turn in tone, imagery, or diction (in a brief and/or nonnarrative poem) imply a plotlike structure to the poem? Is it fair to say that such turns prove that plot is inescapable, even when no discrete events are narrated? Such questions point to the inherent linearity of the language arts: some poems are small enough to be fixed on the page like a framed picture, and of course poems, plays, novels, and essays can always be reread, excerpted out of sequence, or read backward, but line by line and word by word (right to left, left to right, or top to bottom) we process text linearly. How does linearity make literature, and poetry in particular, different from, say, a photograph or a sculpture, but similar to a piece of music? How does it guarantee that we will look for turns in meaning—narrative, imagistic, tonal, etc.—in any text?

Jonson, "To the Reader": This poem represents just about the bare minimum in English verse—two terse lines suited for epigraph, but containing almost no imagery, argument, or development in their simple plea. Yet, can your students find an important turning point in the second line's caesura? What possibilities are being set parallel to each other? What confusion are we being warned against?

Edward Thomas, "As the team's head brass": This poem is almost irresistible as a choice for discussing turning points. The entire text is built on the trope of (re)turning and cyclicity, from the first line's semaphoric image, "As the team's head brass flashed out on the turn." Ask your students to describe how a team of horses or oxen plows a field, perhaps even having someone draw the furrows on the board. The idea is to get them to notice the way the lines turn and return, the very pattern that the poem's speaker observes from his stationary point in the text. Ask them then what other images of turn and return the poem features. What turning points in the attitude of the speaker can they find? How does the poem hinge on the brief dialogue between plowman and speaker just as the furrow hinges on the turn of the plow? You might also point out that the ancient Greeks wrote their texts neither simply left to right or vice versa, but turning and reversing from line to line. In what sense do poetic lines still connect rather than break from line to line? (See also section 1.1.C, "Enjambment and End-Stopped Lines.")

Stevens, "Thirteen Ways of Looking at a Blackbird": In this fragmentary procession of images, each turn is an abrupt shift in figurative perspective. Does the poem progress from image to image? Is there a single central turning point, a fulcrum to be found? Does this poem defy linearity with its discrete pieces like picture shards?

Ashbery, "Brute Image": Ashbery's poems are known for reading like arguments that undo themselves as they go, so that the reader cannot construct a coherent whole despite feeling as though, for any few lines at a time, the poem's syntax is unproblematic. What turning points serve to baffle the reader in this poem and what self-referential passages does the text seem to contain? This self-deconstructing argument demonstrates another way in which the linearity of language art can be defied if not denied. (See the Stevens poem above.)

Adcock, "The Ex-Queen Among the Astronomers": How does the poem turn between the third and fourth, then fifth and sixth stanzas?

Lee, "Persimmons" *CD-ROM Link: The back and forth of languages, sexes, and generations provide a series of turns and counterturns in this poem. Ask your students to identify as many as they can and perhaps to rank them in order of importance. This ranking can even be arranged in a tree on the board as a kind of simple parsing exercise in protostructuralist analysis of a text.

D. *Two-Stanza Poems and Other Absent Middles*

Poems with only two stanzas raise the possibility that some poems do not have middles at all. An exercise: ask students to sketch out in prose a middle stanza, and consider how the insertion of this middle alters the poem's effect and meaning. You might also teach some sonnets in this context: which sonnets are conceived of in two sections, which in three or more?

Anonymous, "Western Wind": One might make up a long story to connect the first two lines with the last two; the cryptic relation between the two halves of the poem makes this a suggestive choice for a student exercise in inserting a middle. What sort of a middle would make this poem less puzzling, and what sort might make it more puzzling?

Shakespeare, "Oh Mistress Mine"

Campion, "When to Her Lute Corinna Sings"

Herrick, "Upon Julia's Clothes": The whole job is done in two stanzas: Julia dressed, Julia undressed. Would a middle stanza show us the process of Julia undressing? Why does Herrick omit this stage? (Or if this poem implies an omitted stanza, should it be a third stanza, perhaps of lovemaking?)

Blake, "The Sick Rose" and "Ah Sun-flower": Compare to Blake's three-stanza poems, such as "The Garden of Love," "I Askéd a Thief," and "Mock on, Mock on, Voltaire, Rousseau." Does the logical development or rhetorical force of the two-stanza poems seem different from that of the three-stanza ones?

Wordsworth, "A Slumber Did My Spirit Seal": What may be understood to have happened between the stanzas? How would the poem's effect be different if there were a middle stanza relating the woman's death?

Dickinson, #49 ("I never lost as much but twice"), #216 ("Safe in their Alabaster Chambers—"), #1129 ("Tell all the Truth but tell it slant—"): Which of these poems seems most as though it could accommodate a middle stanza? Which of Dickinson's three-stanza poems would suffer least, and which most, from the omission of its middle stanza? (Questions like these probably have no right answer, but in order to come up with a defensible choice, students would have to read and compare the poems with considerable care.)

Housman, "Crossing Alone the Nighted Ferry"

Sassoon, " 'They' "

Lewis, "Where are the War Poets?"

Auden, "In Memory of W. B. Yeats" *CD-ROM Link

Palmer, "Fifth Prose"

3.4 Closure

It would be useful to have an index of last lines as well as of first ones, and not simply because for some poems we are more likely to remember the last line than the first. A poem can end with a bang or a whimper, with a crash of cymbals or a gentle decrescendo, with a snappy answer, a desperate outcry, or a gentle fading of the voice. The finality, complexity, or overall effect of a poem's ending is not simply a product of the last line, of course; discussing poetic closure inevitably touches upon larger matters of rhetorical development and structure (see Barbara Herrnstein Smith's *Poetic Closure: A Study of How Poems End* [Chicago: University of Chicago Press, 1968]). A poet may bring a poem to an end by breaking its pattern (particularly in a stanzaic poem that could very well just go on and on with the addition of more stanzas), or by alluding to other kinds of endings or kinds of cessation (death, sleep, night, winter). Bringing attention to closure can also be a way to focus a lesson on a single poet: students may more easily notice other threads that run through a poet's work if you ask them to identify habits that the poet displays in ending his or her poems.

Chaucer, "Complaint to His Purse": The closing "Envoy" sends the poem along to the man who could do something about the state of the poet's purse. Does this contradict the poet's opening claim that he is complaining only to his purse "and to noon other wight"?

Southwell, "The Burning Babe": The last line's delayed remembrance is almost like the solving of a riddle; does it explain all the strange happenings in the poem?

Whitman, "Vigil Strange I Kept on the Field One Night": Why does the devastatingly blunt last line bring the poem to such a solid ending? Because it talks about the finality of burial? Because it is considerably shorter than any other line in the poem?

Yeats, "Among School Children": Yeats often ends poems with questions, as in "The Wild Swans at Coole," "The Second Coming," "Leda and the Swan." (See section 3.4.A, "Bangs, Whimpers, and Rhetorical Questions, below.)

Robinson, "Richard Cory": The ending of the poem is also the end of Richard Cory; compare with the ending of Robinson's "Miniver Cheevy," which startles because it tells us something we did not know about the title character, but concludes with a continuing, not a decisive, action (though one suspects that Miniver's drinking is just a slow way of putting a bullet through his head).

Frost, "Stopping By Woods on a Snowy Evening": Why is the last line repeated? Frost excels at the deceptively simple ending; compare "The Road Not Taken"—has the chosen road made "all the difference" when the roads look so much alike? A decrescendo, or sense of a "diminished thing," ends not only "The Oven Bird" but also "Design," "Come In," and "The Most of It."

Bishop, "The Fish": What is the effect of the way in which the fish, and the poem about it, are "let go" in the same moment?

A. *Bangs, Whimpers, and Rhetorical Questions*

Poetic closure generally takes one of three forms. The poem may end dramatically, with greater emphasis on the final lines or phrases than on those preceding. This can be accomplished with an emphatic closing rhyme, often accompanying a startling image or rhetorical twist, as in the couplet close of **Donne's** Holy Sonnet 14 ("Batter my heart, three-personed God"): "for I / Except you 'enthrall me, never shall be free, / Nor ever chaste, except you ravish me." Or it can be accomplished by an exhortation, as at the end of **Tennyson's** "Ulysses": "To strive, to seek, to find, and not to yield" (*CD-ROM Link). Or the poem may end on a deliberately softer, more uncertain note, as in **Keats's** conclusion of "To Autumn," wherein the rhyme pattern is such as to be fainter on the final line than on the previous two, and the image is one of ambiguous suspension: "Hedge crickets sing; and now with treble soft / The redbreast whistles from a garden-croft; / And gathering swallows twitter in the skies." The gentle melancholy of this ending is later imitated by **Stevens** in his "Sunday Morning," and **Stevens** actually goes so far as to put the very word "ambiguous" into his final lines: "At evening, casual flocks of pigeons make / Ambiguous undulations as they sink, / Downward to darkness, on extended wings" (*CD-ROM Link). From the Renaissance through the Victorian era, dramatic endings were rather more the norm; in the twentieth century, the challenge of concluding a poem has frequently been, as **Frost** put it, "what to make of a diminished thing." Often, however, poets chose to conclude with neither a bang nor a whimper, but with a rhetorical question. **Yeats's** "Among School Children" closes with the couplet, "O body swayed to music, O brightening glance, / How can we know the dancer from the dance?" As Paul de Man pointed out, the question is permanently irresolveable—we cannot even be sure whether the question is intended to express the impossibility of knowing its answer or to stir readers to seek out that answer. Among the following poems, which conclude emphatically, which diffidently, and which with questions? You might ask your students to explain what makes a particular conclusion sound dramatic or hesitant. You could also bring up the issue of how the different kinds of closure are (in)appropriate to a particular poem. An exercise: have your students turn a dramatic ending into a quiet anticlimax (and vice versa), then have them turn question endings into statements (and vice versa). What effects do they notice on the apparent meaning or tone of the poem?

Mew, "The Farmer's Bride"
H.D. From "The Walls Do Not Fall"
Sassoon, "Everyone Sang"
Lowry, "Delirium in Vera Cruz"
Larkin, "MCMXIV" and "Talking in Bed"
Porter, "A Consumer's Report"
Seeger, "Where Have All the Flowers Gone?"
Kenney, "Apples on Champlain"
Duffy, "Warming Her Pearls"
Lee, "Persimmons" *CD-ROM Link
Zarin, "Song"

B. *Poems that Resist or Subvert Their Own Closure*

Some poems are like the fabled universal serpent, the Ouroboros, that nestled with its tail in its mouth. What is the effect of repeating (even when not quite exactly) the first line in the last? When the first line comes around again in the last, how are we better prepared to make sense of it? Or how may our understanding of the first line be undermined, deepened, or qualified when it occurs in the last line? When the reading of a poem seems circular, how does this defy the linearity of the medium? In this context, you might also wish to teach the villanelle (see section 4.2.C), as a conventional pattern dictating that the poem's ending must repeat its beginning. On the other hand, a poem with such a circular structure may be seen as more rather than less tightly closed, and even poems that do not lead us explicitly back to their openings may find some other way to resist our expectation that a poem has a fixed and distinct beginning, middle, and end. Riddles, non sequiturs, and statements orthogonal to the rest of the text can all create a sense of permanent openness rather than closure, as can formal devices such as **Palmer's** anaphoric catalog of phrases borrowed from fairy tales in "Of this cloth doll which"—many more of the potentially infinite number of further phrases could be tacked on to the end by the readers themselves: "to Finally it sneezed / to The boat tipped over / to Flesh and blood / to Out of the whale's mouth." As an exercise, have your students expand this series of phrases with other tags from fairy tales. Why does **Palmer** end the list where he does? What makes this a poem? (You might want to take this opportunity to bring up the link between poetry and chant. See also section 4.5.B, "Charts and Prayers.")

Blake, "The Tyger": A special version of closure by question. How does this differ from a closing rhetorical question that was not also the opening gambit of the poem?
Byron, "When We Two Parted"
Dickinson, #745 ("Renunciation—is a piercing Virtue—")

Stevens, "Of Mere Being"
Williams, "The Dance"
MacNeice, "The Sunlight on the Garden"
Lowry, "Strange Type"
O'Hara, "Why I Am Not a Painter"
Palmer, "Fifth Prose"

3.5 Framing Devices

Some poems tell, or purport to tell, a story within a story, or begin in the words of a speaker who announces that he or she will recount a secondhand report of a tale. Such framing devices put the poem at one remove from immediacy, as well as invite reflection on the nature of poetic narration and poetic veracity in general. Sometimes the frames are left incomplete or unclosed—that is, the "I" who is telling the tale told to him or her never returns when the tale is complete, as though the "I" became wholly absorbed in the voice whose report he or she is repeating ("Ozymandias"). In other cases, the end of the poem is signaled by the conclusion of the tale-within-the-poem and by some account of the response of the original speaker to what he or she has heard ("The Rime of the Ancient Mariner"). Sometimes the framing narration or prologue and the tale-within-the-poem or portion within the frame will be in different meters ("On the Morning of Christ's Nativity"). See also section 7.5 "Cited or Interpolated Voices."

Anonymous, From *Pearl*

Coleridge, "The Rime of the Ancient Mariner": What is the function of the poem's frame or prologue (lines 1–40), in which we learn that the Mariner's tale is narrated to the Wedding Guest? How is our reading of the entire poem colored by knowing that it is narrated to a reluctant listener who is detained from his business elsewhere? How is the frame closed at the end?

Shelley, "Ozymandias": Why is the account of Ozymandias introduced as a secondhand report from a "traveler from an antique land"? Why does the "I" of the poem not return at the end? How would the whole poem be different if its frame were closed, that is, if it ended with something like, "And that's the story the traveler told me"?

Tennyson, "The Lotos-Eaters": What is the function of the introduction to the "Choric Song"? How would the poem be different if the initial voice of the storyteller were to return at the end of the "Choric Song"?

Yeats, "Under Ben Bulben": In what sense does the first section, ending with "Here's the gist of what they mean" (line 12), function as a narrative or explanatory frame for the poem?

Moss, "The Persistence of Song"
Dove, "Parsley" *CD-ROM Link

3.6 Refrains

Some refrains are simply nonsense syllables enabling everyone to sing along between the stanzas (**Shakespeare's** "It Was a Lover and His Lass"), but others may perform a wide range of functions and have many different relations to the stanzas they punctuate or separate. A refrain may take the form of a repeated prayer or intercession (**Kipling's** "Recessional"), a statement that counters or outweighs the stanzas (the anonymous lyric "There Is a Lady Sweet and Kind"), an analogy that unites the varied matter of the individual stanzas (**Yeats's** "Long-Legged Fly"), a response from or the interpolation of a new voice (**Hardy's** "The Ruined Maid"). Some refrains accumulate significance as they recur after each stanza. Each time such a refrain comes around, how has it become richer (more resonant, more confusing, more suggestive)? Other refrains may seem to be drained of meaning through repetition. An exercise: have students invent a refrain for a short poem in stanzas that doesn't have one; likely candidates—for different reasons—include **Herrick's** "To the Virgins, to Make Much of Time," **Lovelace's** "To Lucasta, Going to the Wars," **Blake's** "Holy Thursday [II.]," **Wordsworth's** "She Dwelt Among the Untrodden Ways," **Housman's** "Loveliest of Trees, the Cherry Now," **Frost's** "Come In," and **Roethke's** "My Papa's Waltz." Or invent several different refrains for the poem, based on different models of how refrains function. Since so many poems with refrains are also song poems, you might want to teach refrain in conjunction with song poetry (see section 4.4, "Forms Composed for Singing").

A. *A Selection of Poems with Refrains*

Anonymous, "Alison"
Anonymous, "Timor Mortis"
William Dunbar, "Lament for the Makaris"
Anonymous, "Tom o' Bedlam's Song"
Queen Elizabeth I, "When I Was Fair and Young" *CD-ROM Link
Gay, Songs from *The Beggar's Opera*, "Air IV"
Tennyson, "The Lady of Shalott" and Songs from *The Princess*
Spirituals, "Go Down, Moses" and "Ezekiel Saw the Wheel"
Kipling, "Recessional"
Yeats, "The Stolen Child" and "Long-Legged Fly"
Auden, "In Memory of W. B. Yeats" *CD-ROM Link
Seeger, "Where Have All the Flowers Gone?"

B. Nonsense or Birdsong Refrains

Anonymous, "The Cuckoo Song"
Nashe, "Spring, the Sweet Spring"
Burns, "Green Grow the Rashes"
Gilbert, "Titwillow"

C. Incremental Refrains

Anonymous, "Lord Randal"
Ralegh, "The Lie"
Spenser, "Epithalamion"
Campion, "My Sweetest Lesbia"
Herrick, "Corinna's Going A-Maying"
Herbert, "Virtue"
Tennyson, "Mariana," "The Splendor Falls," "Tears, Idle Tears"
Hardy, "The Ruined Maid"
Kipling, "Tommy"
Bogan, "Song for the Last Act"
MacNeice, "Bagpipe Music"
Fenton, "In Paris with You"

D. Linked Refrains

Gilbert, "Titwillow"
Parker, "One Perfect Rose"
Muldoon, "Milkweed and Monarch"

3.7 Lists

Poems that list things are a good way to make palpable the various kinds of organizing grids that poetic form places on words. An exercise: have students find or make a list of fifteen or so words or items (a shopping list, ingredients in a recipe or on a package label, list of courses, list of states or presidents, chemical elements, roll of students in the class, etc.), and arrange them in five lines or so, perhaps retaining an alphabetical, chronological, or other order, and perhaps reshuffling them to bring out likenesses of sound or other similarities. How does arranging these words in lines add order, and suggest some affinities among the words or items grouped in a single line? How does arranging the words in lines also suggest increased possibilities for randomness, or new possibilities for rearrangement? Or rearrange the items cataloged in one of the poems below in some other order (alphabetical, according to number of syllables, etc.). How does the significance of the list—and of the entire listing process—change when the words are listed in a new sequence? Consider the list of poems below. Which of these poems seem to be taking an inventory not of things but of the words that name the things?

Herrick, "The Argument of His Book": What is the order of items in this versified table of contents? What unifies the poem, when each line seems to have its own logic and rationale (the first line lists words that begin with "b," the second line lists the spring and summer months in order, the third lists the paraphernalia of country festivals, and so on)? How many of the topics listed here are represented in the selections from Herrick in the anthology?
Herbert, "Prayer (I)": Is there a discernible order to this series of analogies for, definitions of, or approximations of prayer? By the end of the poem, is the difficult, many-sided phenomenon called "prayer" at last "something understood"?
E. B. Browning, *Sonnets from the Portuguese*, 43 ("How do I love thee? Let me count the ways")
Whitman, "Beat! Beat! Drums!"
Gilbert, "I Am the Very Model of a Modern Major-General"
Hopkins, "Pied Beauty"
Stevens, "Thirteen Ways of Looking at a Blackbird"
Parker, "Résumé"
Graves, "Warning to Children"
L. Hughes, "The Negro Speaks of Rivers"
Kinnell, "The Correspondence School Instructor Says Goodbye to His Poetry Students"
Donald Hall, From "The One Day," "Prophecy"
Corn, "Contemporary Culture and the Letter 'K' "
Palmer, "Of this cloth doll which"
Graham, "Opulence"
Zarin, "Song"

3.8 Other Structures of Repetition and Variation

There are many ways a poem can repeat and many things it can repeat, such as words, phrases, rhythms, sounds, whole stanzas. The first two sections of this Guide—on versification and stanza forms—are concerned with kinds of repetition basic to all poetry. Probably every poem in the anthology repeats something; this list is merely an introductory gathering to illustrate some of the kinds of repetition of words or phrases within poems—excluding refrains, which are listed above (in section 3.6, "Refrains").

Anonymous, "I Sing of a Maiden"

Brontë, "Remembrance": A good introduction to a wide range of repetitive effects in poetry. Have students note repeated words, phrases, sounds. How do these repetitions help to register the speaker's attitude toward remembrance?

Stevens, "Thirteen Ways of Looking at a Blackbird" and "Waving Adieu, Adieu, Adieu"

S. Smith, "Pretty"

Jarrell, "A Man Meets a Woman in the Street"

Moss, "The Persistence of Song"

Fenton, "In Paris with You"

CHAPTER 4

Forms

4.1 Sonnets

Binding, challenging, and brief, the sonnet form has long been a place for meditations on the very nature of poetic form and its place in the history of poetry. No latter-day poet can write a sonnet without acknowledging in some way—paying homage to, challenging, rethinking—the long line of memorable sonnets that have already been written. With that in mind, here are a few sonnets whose subject matter is the sonnet:

Drayton, "To the Reader of these Sonnets"
Wordsworth, "Nuns Fret Not at Their Convent's Narrow Room" and "Scorn Not the Sonnet"
Keats, "On the Sonnet"
D. G. Rossetti, "A Sonnet"

A. *Petrarchan and Shakespearean Sonnets (See "Versification")*

Students usually remember the formulaic distinction between Petrarchan (or Italian) and Shakespearean (or English) sonnet forms quite easily. Beyond the simple octave-sestet vs. quatrains-couplet distinctions, however, it may be worth pointing out that the couplet closure in the Shakespearean sonnet shows the influence of the witty epigram on the conventional Petrarchan lyric and allows for a very different sort of turn at poem's end: the couplets are often paradoxical or ironic or invert the argument of the three quatrains, for instance. Rather than stop at itemizing the mechanical differences between the forms, encourage the students to compare samples of each and articulate their own perception of the differences between them. (See also sections 2.1, "Couplets and Heroic Couplets"; 2.3, "Four-Line Stanzas: Quatrains"; 3.4, "Closure"; and 4.2.A, "Epigram.")

Ralegh, "A Vision upon the Fairy Queen"
Spenser, From *Amoretti*
Sir Philip Sidney, From *Astrophil and Stella*
Shakespeare, Sonnets
Jonson, "A Sonnet to the Noble Lady, the Lady Mary Wroth"
Wroth, From "A Crown of Sonnets Dedicated to Love"
Longfellow, "The Cross of Snow"
Very, "The Dead" and "The Lost"
Tuckerman, From Sonnets, Second Series
Frost, "Acquainted with the Night," "Design," and "The Silken Tent"
Cummings, "the Cambridge ladies who live in furnished souls"
Lowry, "Delirium in Vera Cruz"

B. Love Sonnets

An instructive and often entertaining workshop for teaching sonnets: have your students read **Shakespeare's** Sonnet 29 and **Spenser's** Sonnet 75 (from the *Amoretti*) before that class date; discuss the history and conventions of the love sonnet with them briefly; have them choose a conventional argument for a love sonnet (i.e., complaint, carpe diem, etc.); break the class up into four groups and have each group work on a quatrain, paying attention to meter and rhyme; as groups finish, have them put their quatrains on the board, while they're still working on them, so that they can borrow freely from each other's work; when the poem is complete, scan it as a whole, ask for revisions from the floor.

Wyatt, "The Long Love, That in My Thought Doth Harbor"
Surrey, "Love, That Doth Reign and Live Within My Thought"
Spenser, From *Amoretti*
Sidney, From *Astrophil and Stella*
Daniel, "Delia," 50 ("Let others sing of knights and paladins")
Drayton, "Idea," 6 ("How many paltry, foolish, painted things")
Shakespeare, Sonnet 138 ("When my love swears that she is made of truth")
Wroth, From "A Crown of Sonnets Dedicated to Love"

Milton, "Methought I Saw"
Keats, "When I Have Fears": Compare to the Elizabethan sonnets that end by praising their own power to grant immortal fame to a mortal love (such as Spenser's Sonnet 75 [*CD-ROM Link]; Drayton's Sonnet 6; and Shakespeare's Sonnets 18, 55, and 65). Since Keats's sonnet ends "Till Love and Fame to nothingness do sink," on what basis can this be considered a love sonnet?
E. B. Browning, *Sonnets from the Portuguese*, 43 ("How do I love thee? Let me count the ways")
Millay, "I, Being Born a Woman and Distressed"

C. *Devotional Sonnets*

Donne, Holy Sonnet, 14 ("Batter my heart, three-personed God")
Herbert, "Sin (I)" and "Prayer (I)"
Milton, "When I Consider How My Light Is Spent"
Longfellow, "The Cross of Snow"
Hopkins, "[Thou Art Indeed Just, Lord . . .]"

D. *Variations on the Sonnet*

How does the range of topics treated in sonnet form expand after the Elizabethan period?

Wordsworth, "It Is a Beauteous Evening"
Shelley, "England in 1819": Compare Wordsworth's sonnet "London, 1802"
Keats, "On First Looking into Chapman's Homer"
Poe, "Sonnet—To Science"
Arnold, "Shakespeare"
Meredith, "Lucifer in Starlight"
C. Rossetti, "In an Artist's Studio"
Hopkins, "[No Worst, There Is None. Pitched Past Pitch of Grief]"
Yeats, "Leda and the Swan"
Frost, "The Oven Bird" and "Design"
Ransom, "Piazza Piece"
Millay, "Euclid Alone Has Looked on Beauty Bare"
Owen, "Anthem for Doomed Youth"
Cummings, "the Cambridge ladies who live in furnished souls"
Crane, "To Emily Dickinson"
Hayden, "Those Winter Sundays"
R. Lowell, "Harriet"
Hill, "Apology for the Revival of Christian Architecture in England"

How has the form of the sonnet been experimented with and altered in the centuries since its Elizabethan heyday? When is a sonnet still a sonnet, and when is it more a "sonnetlike" poem than a sonnet? This again raises the issue of the historical evolution and polymorphousness of any generic form, as did the questions on common meter (see section 1.2.C.).

P. Sidney, "What Length of Verse?": This satiric poem, in "poulter's measure," parodies the sonneteering of Elizabethan poetasters (see also section 1.2.D, "Other Iambic Meters"). For Sidney, clearly, the variations that many introduced into the form were signs of their incompetence. This raises the question of whether following a form strictly is a measure of great craft or lack of originality; conversely, is experimentation with form a sign of a gifted and daring imagination or of an incapacity to handle the strict rules with grace? These are old, recurring questions: early-eighteenth-century poets scorned the rougher metrics of prior centuries, for instance, while late-eighteenth- and early-19th-century poets then scorned in turn the euphonious smoothness of "numbers" that the previous century had perfected. You might not want to introduce this debate to beginning students of poetry, but if you do you may find that they already hold surprisingly spirited opinions on the subject.

Meredith, *Modern Love*, 30 ("What are we first? First, animals; and next"): Sixteen lines long, the poems in *Modern Love* do not fit the sonnet form exactly, of course; but as the last line of this one suggests, they acknowledge in complex ways the tradition of the love sonnet, and the tale of a troubled love, often a love triangle, narrated in such Renaissance sequences as Shakespeare's sonnets.

Cummings, "'next to of course god america i": This poem actually observes the conventions of traditional sonnet form quite closely, yet many readers are slow to recognize it as a sonnet. What distracts us from the form? Is this a variation on the form or a thinly disguised conventional sonnet?

Brooks, "the rites for Cousin Vit"

Heaney, "A Dream of Jealousy"

4.2 Other Influential Fixed Forms

A. *Epigram*

Rooted in the classical inscriptive distich as preserved in the Greek Anthology, the epigram first entered English poetry through the new medium of print in the fifteenth century. It became both a popular form in its own right and an influence on a number of other forms as well. The

Shakespearean sonnet, the heroic couplet, even the English nursery rhyme betray its impact. Witty, compact, built around a single clever turn of phrase—usually sprung in the second line of a rhyming couplet, sometimes in the third or fourth line of a quatrain—the epigram has been the principle vehicle of satiric verse in the English language. However, since the Romantic era, the epigram has been reduced in status to witticism, mere versifying, not true poetry. Students to this day find epigrams both enjoyable and puzzling, as they are unsure what they are supposed to "do" with them. An exercise: have your students try to predict the second line of two or three of the small selection of epigrams below. Alternatively or additionally, have the students cooperatively write epigrams of their own in small groups. This is a form usually better understood by attempting than by analyzing, as the tools of close reading are of little help in such minimalist, impersonal pieces.

Jonson, "On Gut"
Pope, "The Rape of the Lock": How are Pope's and Johnson's (below) longer satiric poems also compendia of epigrams?
Johnson, "The Vanity of Human Wishes"
Emerson, "Intellect"
Dickinson, #1763 ("Fame is a bee")
MacDiarmid, "Another Epitaph on an Army of Mercenaries"
Lewis, "Where are the War Poets?"
Momaday, "The Gift" and "Two Figures"

B. Limerick (See "Versification")

One of the many light-verse cousins of the satirical epigram is the limerick, a form both unusual and nearly universally known among speakers of English. There is such a vast popular, semi-oral culture of anonymously composed and circulated ribald limericks that many people associate the limerick itself with sexual humor of the bathroom-wall variety. This anthology contains samples of the work of the form's originator, Edward Lear, the premier Victorian composer of light verse. If appropriate, you might ask your students to compose their own limericks.

Lear, "There Was an Old Man with a Beard," "There Was an Old Man in a Tree," and "There Was an Old Man Who Supposed"

C. Villanelle (See "Versification")

The villanelle could be taught in conjunction with couplets, as the pattern of the villanelle might be thought of as an intricate delaying of the coming together of the first and third lines as a couplet closing the poem: what transformations and groupings must these two lines each undergo or participate in separately before they can act as a couplet? How does this delay reinforce the villanelle's sense of finality?

Roethke, "The Waking": How is the poem different if you put a comma in line 3 after "going," or after "learn"? That is, at what point in this poem are we likely to decide that the richly ambiguous third line means "I learn wherever it is I have to go, simply by the act of going there," and not "I learn (whatever it is I learn) by going where I know I must go?" Or does the line hover somewhere between those two meanings? If so, how does the pattern of the villanelle help to keep both senses of the line in play?

Bishop, "One Art"

D. Thomas, "Do Not Go Gentle into That Good Night": Although the crucial first and third lines of Thomas's villanelle do not share the shimmering ambiguities of Roethke's lines, how do they undergo changes of meaning as they recur? Where do the lines' imperatives become indicative verbs, and what is the effect of this shift?

Muldoon, "Milkweed and Monarch"

Dove, "Parsley," part 1 *CD-ROM Link

D. Sestina (See "Versification")

Although an eccentric, difficult, and rare form, the sestina is useful for teaching the way poets can alter and refine the meaning of a word through repeating it in different contexts throughout a poem. The changing contexts of the end words of a sestina make the words accumulate a series of associations much as rhyme often does—that is, the changing partners a word accumulates in a rhyme scheme create a halo of associations for that word. A successful sestina is such a display of virtuosity that it reminds us that "poetry" is literally "making," and that a poem can be an intricately crafted artifact, a made thing, as well as an expressive utterance, a heartfelt response. Jon Stallworthy suggests that in writing such complicated forms as the sestina and the villanelle, poets aim for "the graceful momentum of good dancing" (see "Versification"); you might ask students to compare these two ways of thinking about elaborately patterned poems: are such poems more like crafted artifacts or like intricate dances? The sestina is so rigid and yet flexible a pattern that it can be a useful form to experiment with as a class exercise: invent a title, choose six words, arrange them in the order in which they must appear at the ends of the lines in six stanzas, and have groups of students collaborate to write a stanza each. To create a Sidneyan sestina, choose six common monosyllabic words of Anglo-Saxon derivation, as Bishop did in her "Sestina" (below).

Sidney, "Ye Goatherd Gods": A double sestina.
Bishop, "Sestina": How do the six recurring words of the sestina figure the repetitive, enclosed household of child and grandmother?
Hecht, "The Book of Yolek"
Ashbery, "The Painter"
Mathews, "Histoire": Mathews manages to use the sestina form to carry the ironic argument of his poem, allowing the monotony and forced fit of the reiterated six "-ism" words to underscore the monotonous, procrustean way in which such words are thrown about in twentieth-century discourse.

4.3 Odes and Elegies

A. *Ode*

The ode, or praise poem, has been popular in English since the Renaissance, although it reached the zenith of its reputation between the mid-eighteenth and nineteenth centuries. For a long while, English poets were under the misapprehension that the classical ode, particularly the Pindaric, was marked by irregular stanza form and irregular meter from stanza to stanza. This made titling a poem an "ode" tantamount to giving it a classically sanctioned license for formal experiment and variety. Odes are often occasional and can be taught along with the poetry of public occasions (see section 7.1.A, "Occasional Poetry").

Finch, "The Spleen"
Gray, "Ode (On the Death of a Favorite Cat, Drowned in a Tub of Goldfishes)": What features of the genre does this mock ode poke fun at?
Collins, "Ode on the Poetical Character"
Wordsworth, "Ode: Intimations of Immortality"
Coleridge, "Dejection: An Ode"
Shelley, "Ode to the West Wind": Is "To a Skylark" an ode? Compare how Shelley addresses these two subjects.
Keats, "Ode to a Nightingale," "Ode on Melancholy," "Ode on a Grecian Urn," and "To Autumn": What common patterns can be found in these diverse poems, known as Keats's "Great Odes"?
Roethke, "I Knew a Woman": "She taught me Turn, and Counter-turn, and Stand" (line 9). What is the point of alluding to lovemaking in terms of an ode?

B. *Elegy*

Poems commemorating a death introduce considerations of how a poem's occasion is related to its structure. How does the loss that prompts the writing of elegies shape a poet's decisions about how to structure the poem and how to follow, reshape, or depart from inherited conventions of writing such poems? How do poems of mourning tend to begin and end? How do poets work toward some consolation that enables them to bring their laments to a satisfying close? What kinds of special demands on language are made by the poet's need to come to terms with death, an experience the poet cannot know directly? How do poems on the death of children differ from poems on the death of spouses, friends, poets, or heads of state? What resources do poets invent to find solace for the loss of a child? of a fellow poet? Poems can be arranged according to the degree and kind of consolation they achieve. Which poets seem inconsolable? How do the ways elegies end, and the kinds of solace they find, shift from earlier, overtly Christian poems to later poems, in which the comforts of faith in an afterlife—or in the reassurances of the elegiac conventions themselves—may no longer be available? The anthology includes a great many elegies; we have compiled first a random introductory list, followed by groupings of elegies for children and poets.

Tichborne, "Tichborne's Elegy": How do the elegance and restraint of Tichborne's figures for his paradoxical condition save the poem from any tinge of maudlin self-pity?

Shakespeare, "Fear No More the Heat o' the Sun": Does the gentle pun at the end of the refrain seem in poor taste for a dirge? Compare to the puns in Jonson's "On My First Son."

Landor, "Rose Aylmer"

Tennyson, "In Memoriam A. H. H.": Compare the endings of sections 7, 50, and 95. How are memories of Hallam linked to particular places and times of day?

Brontë, "Remembrance"

Whitman, "When Lilacs Last in the Dooryard Bloom'd": How does Whitman combine a sense of personal and national mourning? Compare the voice of the bird in section 14 with other imagined voices in elegies, as in Wordsworth's "Three Years She Grew" and Milton's "Lycidas."

Hardy, "Thoughts of Phena"

Atwood, "Flowers"

ELEGIES FOR CHILDREN

Anonymous, From *Pearl*

Jonson, "On My First Daughter" and "On My First Son": How do Jonson's strategies of consolation differ for a male child and a female child? See Bradstreet, "The Author to Her Book," for another comparison of a child to a poem.

Philips, "Epitaph"

Wordsworth, "Three Years She Grew": What prompts the invention of the voice of Nature?

Housman, "To an Athlete Dying Young": Its ascribing to the dead a Hellenic, heroic end makes this poem a good contrast to elegies with a more Christian consolation.

Ransom, "Bells for John Whiteside's Daughter": What is the function of the vignette in stanzas 2–4 of the girl chasing the geese? Compare this passage to Nature's description of the girl in Wordsworth, "Three Years She Grew" and "Elegiac Stanzas." The latter poem seems occasioned as much by another work of art as by a death. How does the death of his brother enable the poet to approve Beaumont's stormy picture of a sight the poet has witnessed as serene?

Roethke, "Elegy for Jane": Compare to Wordsworth's and Ransom's elegies for girls: why does Roethke see Jane as a bird? Why is consolation so difficult for him to find?

D. Thomas, "A Refusal to Mourn the Death, by Fire, of a Child in London": In what sense is Thomas's refusal a rebuttal to other poems on this list? Why does he see elegy as a kind of blasphemy?

Brooks, "the rites for Cousin Vit"

Elegies for Poets

W. Dunbar, "Lament for the Makaris": Not all elegies for poets insist that their verse makes them immortal. In Dunbar's list of the poets whom death has mown down, why is there so little sense that their lines prolong their lives?

Surrey, "Wyatt Resteth Here": As in Jonson's elegy for Shakespeare (below), elegies for poets often undertake rankings of poetic greatness. What role did poetic rivalry play in Wyatt's art? Compare the nationalistic strain in a number of these Renaissance elegies: the insistence that these poets bring glory to Britain reminds us that writers of verse in English often felt themselves inferior to classical and Continental poets.

Jonson, "To the Memory of My Beloved, the Author Mr. William Shakespeare": What is the effect of the hesitancies and false starts of lines 1–17? How would our sense of the relation between Shakespeare and Jonson be different if the poem began with "Soul of the Age!"? Why does Jonson insist that Shakespeare's greatness is as much "Art" as "Nature"? Along with this poem assign some of Shakespeare's songs and sonnets, and ask the class to consider what features of them Jonson might have admired, on the basis of his elegy. Compare Jonson's praise with what Shakespeare says of his own poetry's immortality (Sonnets 55, 65).

Herrick, "An Ode for Him": What is the effect of the increasing line lengths in each stanza?

Carew, "An Elegy upon the Death of the Dean of Paul's, Dr. John Donne": Assign some of Donne's poems and ask the class to find examples of the kinds of purgation and weeding out of poetic language that Carew's elegy ascribes to Donne. What Donnelike touches in Carew's poem attest to the truth of his claims about Donne's verse? How does Carew handle the tricky assignment of paying tribute to a poet who began writing secular, often erotic, poetry, but who ended his career as a priest and religious poet?

Milton, "Lycidas": How are the strategies of consolation different for the death of a young poet (here, Edward King; Dryden's elegy for Oldham; Shelley's for Keats) and the death of an older one who has fulfilled his promise (Surrey on Wyatt, Jonson on Shakespeare, Carew on Donne)? How does Milton make use of the special circumstances of King's death by drowning? Consider the progression of kinds of "false surmise" (line 153) and compare them to those in other poems in this group.

Dryden, "To the Memory of Mr. Oldham": What is the effect of the alexandrines (six-beat lines or hexameters) at lines 21 and 25? At the beginning of the poem, Oldham and Dryden seem to be almost twins: how does the distance between them increase as the poem progresses?

Shelley, "Adonais": This compendium of elegiac devices is perhaps best taught toward the end of a unit on the elegy. Does Shelley give us a sense of what Keats was like as a poet, in the way Carew does for Donne? Compare with other poems on the early death of a poet ("Lycidas," "To the Memory of Mr. Oldham").

Auden, "In Memory of W. B. Yeats" *CD-ROM Link

Berryman, Dream Song 324, "An Elegy for W. C. W., The Lovely Man": What connections are made between Williams's two professions, poet and physician? How does Berryman revise the idea of "envy" common to these elegies for poets? How do the other Dream Songs in the anthology suggest why Berryman envies less Williams's virtuosity than his being beyond the need to prove it?

4.4 Forms Composed for Singing

What makes some poems more suitable than others to be set to music or sung? Listed here, among other songs, are most of the poems that are titled "Song"; but this label clearly means different things in different instances. So many poets with highly varied designs and ambitions have called their works "songs"—from *Songs of Innocence* and *Songs of Experience* to "Song of Myself" (*CD-ROM Link) to "The Love Song of J. Alfred Prufrock" to

"The Dream Songs"—that we may wonder what power and resonance such a label is thought to hold. Which features of traditional song—Renaissance love lyrics, or **Dryden's** "A Song for St. Cecilia's Day," or lyrics commissioned for a musical setting—do **Whitman** and **Eliot** and **Ashbery** wish to invoke when they call their poems "songs"?

Anonymous, "Fowls in the Frith"
Anonymous, "I Am of Ireland"
Anonymous, "Fine Knacks for Ladies"
Shakespeare, "It Was a Lover and His Lass": This poem is marked for singing by its recurrent nonsense refrain, a mere place-filler that serves to carry the tune and enables listeners to join in whether they know the words to the song or not.
Campion, "My Sweetest Lesbia" and all other Campion selections: These poems were written to be sung to lute accompaniment: what features do they share that make them singable? In which poems does Campion seem to have been hard pressed to make all the stanzas fit equally well into the same tune? In "When to Her Lute Corinna Sings," what is the relation between voice and instrument? Compare Corinna as a singer with Campion's "Rose-cheeked Laura," and her "beauty's / silent music."
Donne, "Song ('Go and catch a falling star')" and "Song ('Sweetest love, I do not go')": What makes these texts better for singing than other poems by Donne in the anthology?
Jonson, "Song: To Celia (I)" and "Song to Celia (II)"
Waller, "Song ('Go, lovely rose!')"
Suckling, "Song ('Why so pale and wan, fond lover?')"
Dryden, "A Song for St. Cecilia's Day"
Blake, "Song ('How sweet I roam'd from field to field')"
Byron, "So We'll Go No More A-Roving": This poem has been set to music.
Lear, "The Owl and the Pussy-Cat": This poem has been set to music.
Christina Rossetti, "Song ('When I am dead, my dearest')"
Tennyson, Songs from *The Princess*
Gilbert, "Titwillow": What marks this poem as something of a parody of Renaissance songs? Which features of the Renaissance selections on this list does it spoof or exaggerate? The challenge they present to the singer is part of the humor of Gilbert's patter songs, which are usually delivered at a breathtaking clip, half sung, half recited, as in "I Am the Very Model of a Modern Major-General."
Eliot, "The Love Song of J. Alfred Prufrock"
Bogan, "Song for the Last Act"
Auden, "Lullaby"

A. *Psalms, Hymns, and Spirituals*

Poets have labeled their poems "hymns" with the same diversity of intent as they call their poems "songs." We have included here all the poems explicitly titled "hymns," but as with the list of "songs," the differences will tend to be more instructive than the similarities. As hymns are generally poems of address to God or a god, they may be taught along with questions of address or apostrophe (see section 7.1). The poems by **Watts, Cowper,** and **Dickinson** may be usefully taught as a group in conjunction with song. What restrictions do **Cowper** and **Watts** labor under in composing religious poems designed to be sung by a congregation to a simple tune? Compare **Cowper's** and **Watts's** hymns for music to the more personal entreaties of **Crashaw** and **Dickinson.** (On hymn meters, see "Versification" and section 1.2.C, "Common Meter and Iambic Tetrameter/Trimeter," above.) The Hebrew psalms are in many respects the ancestors of English hymns, and many hymns are based directly on a psalm. Spirituals are a special, African-American variety of hymn, drawing on both biblical psalms and traditional English hymnody but also rooted in the suffering of slavery and bearing the traces of African and African-American oral culture. An exercise: bring in copies of Psalm 23 and Psalm 58 in contemporary translation; have students compare their structures to that of the translations of the psalms in *The Massachusetts Bay Psalm Book* as well as to the separate translations of Psalm 58. Then compare the translated psalms to other hymns and to spirituals. What common elements bind these forms, aside from the obvious fact of religious faith? What is unique to psalms and spirituals? How similar are English hymns and African-American spirituals to ballads? (See also section 1.3.C, "Parallel Verse," above and section 4.4.B, "Ballads," below.) Another discussion exercise: compare a hymn with one of **Donne's** Holy Sonnets and with one of **Campion's** song lyrics, and ask your students with which form the hymn has more in common and why. This may provide entry into a discussion of form vs. content in the determination of genre: should we group poems by subject matter, attitude, or physical form? How is it that the same physical form appropriate to "Amazing Grace" also fits "The Yellow Rose of Texas," "The House of the Rising Sun," and Dickinson's #712 ("Because I could not stop for Death—")? (See section 1.2.C, "Common Meter and Iambic Tetrameter/Trimeter.") Meaning can seem to overwhelm form on the page, but when the poem is set to music, the feel of the tune can overwhelm both. Have your students try to explain why, as a way of getting them to think critically about the interrelationships of physical and semantic elements in poetry.

Cædmon's "Hymn"
M. Sidney, "Psalm 58"

Crashaw, "A Hymn to the Name and Honor of the Admirable Saint Teresa"
The Massachusetts Bay Psalm Book, "Psalm 58"
Watts, "Our God, Our Help": What features of this hymn (in common meter) would make it easy for a congregation to sing it in unison?
Smart, "Psalm 58"
Cowper, "Olney Hymns": Is Cowper's or Watts's hymn easier to sing? How do both Cowper and Watts give the congregation time to catch their breath while singing? Which hymn is easier for the worshippers to understand while they are singing it?
Blake, "And Did Those Feet"
Shelley, "Hymn to Intellectual Beauty": What conventions of address and entreaty does Shelley borrow from religious hymns?
Emerson, "Concord Hymn"
Howe, "Battle-Hymn of the Republic"
Spirituals, "Go Down, Moses" and "Ezekiel Saw the Wheel"
Dickinson, #258 ("There's a certain Slant of light") and #1129 ("Tell all the Truth but tell it slant—"): Compared to the straightforwardness of the poems by Cowper and Watts, the heterodox, "slant" nature of Dickinson's private hymns (or the degree to which this label is accurate) becomes easier to see. Why can we imagine a congregation singing Watts's hymn, but not Dickinson's poems, although the latter are written almost entirely in some form of hymn meter? (Yet Aaron Copland has set some of Dickinson's poems to music.)

B. Ballads (See "Versification")

How do ballads narrate events? Why do ballads often begin at the climax, or even aftermath, of their stories? Compare the modern ballads of **Housman** and **Auden** with the anonymous folk or popular ballads. In what ways do these literary ballads—written to be read, not sung—allude to the conventions of popular ballads? In what ways do they suggest that the world has changed so radically, since the days of "Lord Randall" and his kin, that the values of folk ballads are no longer tenable? (This conjunction of old and new could also be taught under the topic of allusion; see section 8.1.)

Anonymous, Early Modern Ballads
Anonymous, "Tom o' Bedlam's Song"
Coleridge, "The Rime of the Ancient Mariner"
Dickinson, #712 ("Because I could not stop for Death—") *CD-ROM Link: In its riddling way of telling a story of a ghoulish courtship, how is this poem somewhat reminiscent of popular ballads like "The Unquiet Grave"?

Housman, "Is my Team Plowing"
Brown, "Slim in Atlanta"
Auden, "As I Walked Out One Evening"
Rukeyser, "Ballad of Orange and Grape"
Brathwaite, "Ancestors"
Seeger, "Where Have All the Flowers Gone?"
Dylan, "Boots of Spanish Leather"

C. Songs from Plays and Longer Poems

Songs can also function as interludes, transitions, and showstoppers within larger poetic and/or dramatic works. This raises the issue of context. Most songs from plays, for instance, were written to be sung in character by one of the players and often illuminate or at least reflect an aspect of that character or of the drama's plot. For discussion, bring in photocopies of a few scenes from **Shakespeare's** plays containing one or two of the songs anthologized here, along with a bit of plot and character summary for each. Have one group of students read the song(s) without having the scenes available, while another group reads the songs in context. Then ask each group to present their interpretation of the song(s). Discuss the reasons for their differences. How important is context to understanding? What about other poems in this anthology—are they also stripped of context in some sense, even if they were published individually? This might be a good discussion during which to foreground questions about anthologies themselves as vehicles for poetry.

Chaucer, "Cantus Troili"
Shakespeare, Songs from the Plays
Milton, Songs from *Comus*
Gay, Songs from *The Beggar's Opera*

4.5 Other Forms Rooted in Oral-Performance Traditions

Besides song lyrics per se and literary lyrics that claim songlike qualities or ancestry, many poems in this anthology show aspects of other forms of oral poetry, including chants, charms, riddles, curses, and prayers. These nonsong traditions of oral verse are nearly as fundamental to poetry in English as song lyrics are. Many of the oldest texts in English verse consist of "kennings," or Anglo-Saxon riddles, and much of the free verse of the past century and more bears a strong family resemblance to chanting.

A. *Kennings, Riddles, and Charms*

Riddles can be a useful category for introducing figurative language (see section 5). Saying one thing in terms of another, or in unfamiliar, novel ways often involves the reader in a game of guessing the comparison.

Anonymous, Riddles
Anonymous, "The Sacrament of the Altar"
Anonymous, "I Sing of a Maiden": The riddle or paradox of a woman who is simultaneously "mother and maiden" suggests that riddles, or the paradoxes they represent, are central to the language of religious poetry.
Anonymous, "I Have a Young Sister": Why do the first three riddles presented within the poem turn on a solution involving a nascent or undeveloped stage of growth, while the fourth involves a state of fulfillment or completion?
Tichborne, "Tichborne's Elegy": How does this series of metaphors for an early death become increasingly paradoxical and riddling?
Herrick, "To Find God"
Dickinson, #986 ("A narrow Fellow in the Grass"): Like a riddle, the poem lists the attributes of the creature (a snake) but does not name him. See also #1463 ("A Route of Evanescence"), usually interpreted as an oblique description of a hummingbird, but also possible to read as a description of the rising sun—"every Blossom on the Bush / Adjusts its tumbled Head." Have your students try reading the poem both ways, perhaps dividing them into two groups to each defend one answer in debate.
C. Rossetti, "Up-Hill": Almost in riddle format of question and answer; the solution becomes clearer as the questions accumulate. In what sense is death itself a riddle?
S. Crane, From *The Black Riders and Other Lines* (LVI)
Swenson, "Cardinal Ideograms"
Raine, "A Martian Sends a Postcard Home": Commonplace objects seen through the eyes of a creature alien to Earth lead to riddling descriptions. When does the Martian's puzzled report accurately tell what life on Earth is like?
Erdrich, "Birth"

B. *Chants and Prayers*

Many hymns can also be considered as prayers or entreaties. We include here prayers not hymnal in form. Chants, in oral cultures, feature hypnotic repetition-with-variation of a small repertoire of similar, emotionally charged phrases: how do some of the free verse poems below suggest such chants?

Herbert, "Prayer (I)"
Taylor, "Meditation 8 ('I kenning through astronomy divine')": Is there a difference between poetry of devout meditation and of prayer?
Smart, "Jubilate Agno ('For I will consider my Cat Jeoffry')"
Burns, "Holy Willie's Prayer"
Whitman, "Song of Myself," section 11 ("Twenty-eight young men bathe by the shore") and "Out of the Cradle Endlessly Rocking"
Hopkins, "[My Own Heart Let Me More Have Pity On]" and "[Thou Art Indeed Just, Lord . . .]"
Stein, From *Stanzas in Meditation*
Sandburg, "Grass"
Ginsberg, "Howl"
Momaday, "The Eagle-Feather Fan"

C. Formulaic Narrative Verse

Beowulf: See also section 4.9.A, "Epic and Mock-Epic."

4.6 Visual Forms

As with onomatopoeia (see section 6.2), which does not make words sound like nonverbal sounds except largely by conventional association between the sound of the word and what the word means, one should be cautious about claiming that the shapes of these oddly formed poems actually picture the objects they describe. **Herbert's** poem looks like wings (and not, say, an hourglass or a dish for an ice-cream sundae) because the title suggests the resemblance and, perhaps, because the poem looks like other poems so shaped and titled. All poems are poem-shaped; some poems are shaped like other shaped poems, and through that association they can be said to look like or be shaped like the things they are about. How do shaped poems explicate the meaning of the things they are shaped like, combining picture and explanatory caption in a shaped text? Assigning students to write their own shaped poems is a good way to sharpen their sense of the physical format of poems generally, and to show how necessity can be the mother of invention when a certain idea must be fit into a prepatterned grid.

A. *Poems Arranged for the Page*

Anonymous, "See! here, my heart"
Hardy, "The Convergence of the Twain": Jon Stallworthy notes (in "Versification") that "the shape of the stanza suggests the iceberg that is the poem's subject." Might it suggest the ship as well?
Birney, "Slug in Woods"
Swenson, "Cardinal Ideograms"

B. *Pattern Poems*

Herrick, "The Pillar of Fame"
Herbert, "Easter Wings" and "The Altar": An exercise: have students, using a typewriter, write a variation on this poem, called "Easter Eggs." What different views of Easter might emerge from a poem whose shape bulges rather than thins in the middle? Another (overnight) exercise: have students compose a poem in the shape of any familiar object, the only requirement being that the poem's content reflect the nature of the object silhouetted by its words.
Hollander, "Swan and Shadow": The poem is about a sight that is transient, hard to see, hard to make out; the poem itself—by virtue of its being a shaped poem—is permanent, an obvious picture, instantly declaring its subject. Is there a way to resolve this contradiction?

4.7 Open Forms (See "Versification")

Poems that are written in forms neither fixed nor patterned are not without form at all. Ask your students how the following free-verse poems differ from each other in form and how that formal difference might affect the tone and meaning of the poems.

Whitman, "When Lilacs Last in the Dooryard Bloom'd"
Stein, From *Stanzas in Meditation*
Sandburg, "Chicago"
W. C. Williams, "This Is Just to Say" and "Poem" *CD-ROM Link
Lawrence, "Snake"
Jeffers, "Carmel Point"
L. Hughes, "Harlem"
Levertov, "Triple Feature"
Ammons, "Corsons Inlet"
Ginsberg, "Howl"
O'Hara, "The Day Lady Died"
Rich, "Diving into the Wreck" *CD-ROM Link

Plath, "Lady Lazarus": How does this rhymed poem also exemplify open form?
Lorde, "Coal"

4.8 Sequences

Poems in sequences represent a curious intermediary stage between book-length poetry and poems of no more than a few hundred lines. Beads on a string, they are neither indissoluble nor wholly independent. Does the fact that these poems come as items in a sequence add to their interest or only weary us with their self-similarity?

A. *Sonnet Sequences*

This anthology prints no sonnet sequences entire: in what ways does the anthology misrepresent these sonnets by isolating them? A question for class discussion: does this anthology misrepresent the sonnets more than it does the other poems it necessarily isolates from the volume or canon from which they were selected?

Spenser, From *Amoretti*
P. Sidney, From *Astrophil and Stella*
Daniel, From *Delia*
Drayton, From *Idea*
Shakespeare, From the Sonnets
Donne, From the Holy Sonnets
Wroth, From "A Crown of Sonnets Dedicated to Love"
Meredith, From *Modern Love*
Tuckerman, From *Sonnets, Second Series*

B. *Other Sequences*

Long poems that are groups of shorter poems, which may be of the same or different lengths and forms, can be represented in the anthology only by selections; the same questions might be asked of the poems listed below as of the sonnets listed above. Why in the modern period have lyric sequences replaced epic as the mode of the long poem? What permutations in tone, attitude, language, etc., are undergone by the speaking voice in these selections? How are these different when the sequence is comprised of identical stanza forms (**Tennyson, Hill**) and when it is composed of sections of varying form and length (**Whitman, Pound**)? The selection from "In Memoriam" perhaps gives the best feel of the challenges and dynamics of lyric sequences.

Whitney, "A Communication Which the Author Had to London, Before She Made Her Will"
Lanyer, From *Salve Deus Rex Judaeorum*
Tennyson, "In Memoriam A. H. H."
Whitman, "Song of Myself" *CD-ROM Link
S. Crane, From *The Black Riders and Other Lines*
Stein, From *Stanzas in Meditation*
Pound, "Hugh Selwyn Mauberley: Life and Contacts"
MacDiarmid, From "In Memoriam James Joyce"
Kavanagh, From "The Great Hunger"
Auden, From "Twelve Songs"
Roethke, "The Lost Son"
Berryman, From "Homage to Mistress Bradstreet" and Dream Songs
Snodgrass, From *Heart's Needle*
Donald Hall, "Prophecy"
Sissman, From "Dying: An Introduction," "Path. Report"
Rich, From "Eastern War Time"
Hill, "Mercian Hymns"
Strand, From *Dark Harbor*, XVI
Heaney, From "Station Island"
Ondaatje, From "Rock Bottom," "(Ends of the Earth)"

4.9 Book-Length Forms

A. *Epic and Mock-Epic*

An introductory course in lyric poetry will rarely have time to study an epic in its entirety; yet selections from an epic can suggest the form's scope and ambitions, and its relation to lyric and other, briefer poetic forms. If classical epics typically narrate the voyages of empire-founders or heroes, Romantic epics transform such national journeys into personal, internal ones (**Wordsworth's** *Prelude*). Should an epic in this century be national (or global?) or autobiographical? A question for class discussion: why hasn't there been an epic poem on the voyage to the moon? or on the risk of nuclear holocaust? (Is it just that our sensibility cannot accommodate the conventions of epic any longer? Or have movies or other forms of culture or entertainment taken over some of the functions and ambitions of epic poetry? What answers to these questions does **Creeley's** "Heroes" suggest?) An exercise: write the opening lines—including invocation to the muse (which muse is part of the problem)—to a modern epic on the moon landings or on nuclear war. Will the result necessarily be mock-epic? (See also section 8.2, "Mythology.")

EPIC

Beowulf
Spenser, From *The Faerie Queene,* Book 1
Milton, From *Paradise Lost,* Book 1 [The Invocation]
Wordsworth, From The *Prelude,* Book I, lines 301–475 ("Fair seedtime had my soul, and I grew up")
Whitman, From "Song of Myself" *CD-ROM Link: Is Whitman's long personal poem an epic? Section 1 ("I celebrate myself, and sing myself") and section 24 ("Walt Whitman, a kosmos, of Manhattan the son") are most pertinent to this issue.
Pound, From *The Cantos,* Canto I ("And then went down to the ship")
Creeley, "Heroes"

MOCK-EPIC

It may be easier to teach the conventions of epic poetry through their parodies than through epics themselves. Among other issues, **Pope's** story of Belinda should raise the question of why the heroes of epic poems are invariably men, and whether an epic poem could be written about a woman.

Pope, "The Rape of the Lock"
Byron, From *Don Juan,* Canto the First

B. Nonnarrative Book-Length Poems

The end of both ages of epic, the oral-formulaic and the literary, has not meant an end to poems of epic ambition and scope. In this century, encyclopedic poems absorbing and (re)presenting myth, history, philosophy, and theology (often as excerpts from heterogeneous texts ranging from letters to advertisements to pop lyrics to scholarly tomes to ouija-board messages) have attempted to perform the traditional epic function, what Pound called "the Tale of the Tribe," but without a unifying narrative.

Skelton, "Phyllip Sparow"
H. D. From "The Walls Do Not Fall"
Eliot, From *Four Quartets,* "III. The Dry Salvages"
MacNeice, From "Autumn Journal"
Berryman, Dream Songs
Merrill, From *The Book of Ephraim*
Snodgrass, From *Heart's Needle*
Strand, From *Dark Harbor,* XVI
Heaney, From "Station Island"

CHAPTER 5

Figuration

Figurative language in poetry is, of course, an enormous topic, and a pervasive one. Most of a poetry course is concerned, on some level, with the ways poems say one thing in terms of another, compare or juxtapose things, or give things a new slant through some kind of gesture that we might call figurative. Some of the poems listed below bring into focus the issue of figurative language because they hang on a single striking metaphor or comparison (**Tennyson, Williams, Merwin**). Others listed below may serve as an introduction to questions of figuration because they take figures of speech as their topic, or explicitly weigh the aptness of metaphors (**Shakespeare, Dickinson**), or propose a shifting series of likenesses (**Burns, Shelley, Keats**).

Shakespeare, Sonnet 18 ("Shall I compare thee to a summer's day?"): Perhaps most fruitfully taught in conjunction with the witty rejection of the Petrarchan comparisons in Sonnet 130 ("My mistress' eyes are nothing like the sun").

Burns, "A Red, Red Rose": A good poem with which to remind students that we understand how to read many metaphors because of conventional associations with the objects that serve as their vehicles. How, for example, do we know that when Burns compares a woman to a rose he is not saying that she has thorns or petals but that she is beautiful and transient? What might a poet have to do to include or emphasize those other features of the rose in the comparison?

Shelley, "To a Skylark"

Keats, "On First Looking into Chapman's Homer"

Tennyson, "Crossing the Bar"

Henry David Thoreau, "I Am a Parcel of Vain Strivings Tied"

Arnold, "The Scholar-Gypsy": Note the final extended metaphor of the "Tyrian-trader" (lines 232ff.): what is the effect of this sudden opening up of the poem to the world beyond the landscape around Oxford?

Dickinson, #1129 ("Tell all the Truth but tell it slant—"): A classic statement of the rationale for metaphor, this poem itself offers a series of comparisons for the poetic act of making comparisons.

Yeats, "Long-Legged Fly": The refrain gives us three chances to test the aptness of the metaphor and to refine our sense of the ground of the comparison: Caesar forms certain (mental) actions in the way a certain kind of fly performs a certain action.

Pound, "In a Station of the Metro"

Cummings, "somewhere i have never travelled, gladly beyond": A good class discussion on metaphor might center around the difference between Burns's "my love's like a red, red rose" and Cummings's more riddling comparison, "the voice of your eyes is deeper than all roses" (line 19).

5.1 Metaphor and Simile

The most familiar of tropes, metaphor and simile are probably already ensconced in the minds of many of your students—that is, students can probably recite some form of the distinction that a metaphor is a direct comparison without using "like" or "as" and a simile is a comparison using "like" or "as." This does not, of course, mean that your students will necessarily spot a metaphor when they see one; often comparisons are visible to students only as similes. For most classes, then, it helps to start training the eye for comparisons of all sorts as soon as possible. Two especially important aspects of figurative-language use: 1) How is this comparison apt, inaccurate, or revealing of bias? and 2) How (well) does this comparison fit into a pattern of figurative and connotative language throughout the poem? Also point out that metaphors, by affirming equivalency, make stronger claims than similes. Ask your class how these two famous comparisons by Shakespeare—"My mistress' eyes are nothing like the sun" and "It is the East! And Juliet is the sun!"—differ, even if we eliminate the negation "nothing" from the simile. An exercise: using blackboard or handouts, present students with halves of comparisons from the short list of poems below and ask them to provide, individually or as a class, whatever metaphor or simile springs to mind. Then have them look up the texts themselves; use this as springboard for a discussion of the two questions about aptness and fitness above.

S. Crane, From "War is Kind": How does the simile "humble as a button" play off multiple ironies implicit in the size, commonness, and domesticity of buttons in the context of war and heroism?
Gunn, "The Missing"
Porter, "A Consumer's Report"
Plath, "Morning Song"
Ondaatje, From "Rock Bottom," "(Ends of the Earth)"
Graham, "Opulence"
Daniel Hall, "Mangosteens"
Zarin, "The Ant Hill"

5.2 Metonymy and Synecdoche

These are the figures of implicit comparison by substitution. They are the figurative terms most difficult for students to grasp effectively—not only are the words difficult and alien, but the linked concepts are harder to differentiate than are those of metaphor and simile. A fairly simple distinction: metonymy substitutes a word for an aspect or quality commonly associated with the word it replaces, whereas synecdoche substitutes the term for a part in place of the term for the whole. It may help to start with commonplace expressions, such as "cradle to grave" (birth to death) for metonymy and "wheels" (car) for synecdoche. An interesting question, then: why substitute associated words or parts-for-wholes in the first place? What poetic qualities emerge from "cradle to grave" and "wheels" that are not apparent in "birth to death" or "car"?

Anonymous, "Fowls in the Frith"
Eliot, "The Love Song of J. Alfred Prufrock": Note how the shadowy female figures in the poem are presented as parts of themselves—voices, eyes, arms "downed with light brown hair." How does this use of synecdoche increase the sense of anxiety, alienation, and fragmentation in the experience of the poem? How does it reduce women to vaguely threatening objects? Is synecdoche necessarily reductive?
Momaday, "The Eagle-Feather Fan"
Muldoon, "Milkweed and Monarch"
Dove, "Parsley" *CD-ROM Link
Soto, "Not Knowing"
Duffy, "Warming Her Pearls"

5.3 Overstatement (Hyperbole) and Understatement (Litotes)

Although nearly self-explanatory, overstatement and understatement are worth calling to students' attention. Much of early English poetry relies on understatement as a form of emphatic trope, giving the poetry its famously stoic quality. Much Renaissance love poetry (indeed, much love poetry to this day) depends upon extravagant hyperbole. All figures, all comparisons alter the way in which we imagine the term compared—how do overstatement and understatement alter our perceptions differently than do metaphor, simile, metonymy, or synecdoche? Make sure your students are aware that these tropes are not mutually exclusive—hyperbolic simile, litotic metonymy, etc., are possible. Often, however, overstatement is employed to attest to the very inadequacy of any comparison, thus laboring to make the item, person, or quality praised appear sui generis, incomparable. An exercise: choose an example of overstatement and have the class turn it into whatever figures it is not already, say, metaphor, metonymy, and synecdoche, by turns. How does each trope change the way we perceive the comparison?

Anonymous, "The Seafarer"
P. Sidney, "Seventh Song"
Daniel, From "Delia," 1 ("Unto the boundless Ocean of thy beauty")
Shakespeare, Sonnet 18 ("Shall I compare thee to a summer's day?")
Donne, "The Sun Rising" and "The Flea"
Marvell, "To His Coy Mistress"
Swift, "The Lady's Dressing Room"
Pope, "The Rape of the Lock"
Gray, "Ode (On the Death of a Favorite Cat, Drowned in a Tub of Goldfishes)": How does this poem employ hyperbole to parody other odes? (See section also 4.3.A, "Ode.")
Goldsmith, "When Lovely Woman Stoops to Folly": Compare this famous bit of hyperbole about female chastity to Eliot's sardonic deflation of same in the typist-and-clerk scene of *The Waste Land*, wherein Goldsmith's injunction "to die!" is traded for the option of putting "another record on the grammophone." Both Goldsmith's melodramatic overstatement and Eliot's ironic understatement of the consequences for a woman engaging in sex outside of marriage are rooted in the stereotypical opposition of virgin and whore. What different attitudes, then, are reflected in the choice of over- or understatement?
Burns, "A Red, Red Rose"
R. Browning, "My Last Duchess": How does understatement convey the duke's menacing, pathological machismo?

Whitman, "Song of Myself," section 24 ("Walt Whitman, a kosmos, of Manhattan the son")
Dickinson, #465 ("I heard a Fly buzz—when I died—")
L. Hughes, "Theme for English B": How does this poem use quiet understatement to emphasize the gulf between the teacher and the student?
Auden, "In Memory of W. B. Yeats" *CD-ROM Link

5.4 Paradox

Paradox is defined by *The New Princeton Encyclopedia of Poetry and Poetics* (Princeton: Princeton UP, 1993) as a "daring statement which unites seeming contradictory words but which on closer examination proves to have unexpected meaning and truth." Using this definition, have your students identify the paradoxes in the following selection and then, perhaps in small groups, work on discovering each paradox's particular "unexpected meaning and truth."

Anonymous, "The Sacrament of the Altar"
Sir Philip Sidney, *Astrophil and Stella*, 63 ("O Grammer rules, ô now your virtues show")
Dickinson, #435 ("Much Madness is divinest Sense—")
Moore, "The Fish": Look carefully at the last two stanzas.

5.5 Personification, Allegory, and Symbolism

Nowadays we tend to feel that the device of giving human attributes to abstract qualities is somewhat clunky or old-fashioned, the stuff of greeting cards or advertisements, where allegorical personages standing for products or their benefits still reign supreme. But as a shorthand procedure for talking about the conflicts of values or the growth of ideas, these devices have remained effective, although in somewhat attenuated forms, up to the present day. (You might wish to discuss with the class to what degree the same logic governs the invention of an allegorical figure of, say, Cleanliness or Purity, and of such commercial characters as Mr. Clean or even of Miss America.) Allegorical personages are often pictured with emblematic props or as holding a characteristic pose: **Collins's** "Truth, in sunny vest arrayed" ("Ode on the Poetical Character"); **Keats's** "Joy, whose hand is ever at his lips / Bidding adieu" ("Ode on Melancholy"); **Emerson's** "Days . . . marching single in an endless file" ("Days"). You might have students invent the appropriate accoutrements and poses for some contemporary, minor, or little-recognized virtues and vices (such as Neatness, Lateness, Consistency, Inefficiency).

Symbolism, meanwhile, may be introduced separately or along with allegory. One straightforward way to introduce symbolism is to bring an ordinary object with rich symbolic possibilities, such as a polished red apple, to class with you. For dramatic effect, you might even choose to simply stand quietly, holding the apple in your hand at the beginning of class until someone asks what you are doing or what the apple is for. At that point, toss the apple to the student and ask him or her what it suggests. Have each student take the apple and state a word or phrase that the student associates with it. Write each suggestion on the board. Now you can introduce your class to the definition of a symbol as a term denoting a concrete object associated with an abstract idea or complex of ideas. Depending on how your syllabus is structured, you could use this opportunity to also introduce connotation and/or allegory, or to build on earlier classes that introduced those terms.

Anonymous, From *Pearl*

Langland, *Piers Plowman*

Spenser, From *The Faerie Queene*, Book 1

Sidney, From *Astrophel and Stella*, 52 ("A strife is grown between Virtue and Love")

Daniel, From "Delia," 6 ("Fair is my love, and cruel as she's fair"): What is lost if lines 9–10 are rewritten to eliminate the personifications? What is the difference between calling Chastity and Beauty "deadly foes" and calling them simply opposed principles, or contradictory values?

Jonson, "Though I Am Young and Cannot Tell"

Milton, "On the Morning of Christ's Nativity" and "On Shakespeare": Allegory can be an occasional effect as well as an overarching mode of presentation, as when Milton gives Shakespeare an allegorical ancestry, "son of Memory, great heir of Fame" (line 5). Compare to other allegorical genealogies, such as the opening of Keats's "Ode on a Grecian Urn," or of Poe's "Sonnet—To Science."

Behn, "Song (Love Arme'd)"

Johnson, "The Vanity of Human Wishes": Several passages accumulate heaps of capitalized abstract nouns that seem to hover between allegorical embodiments of the qualities named ("captive Science" [line 144], "misty Doubt" [line 146], "hissing Infamy" [line 342]) and simple descriptions of those qualities ("afflicted Worth" [line 310], "neglected Virtue" [line 333]).

Collins, "Ode on the Poetical Character"

Barbauld, "Life"

Keats, "Ode on Melancholy": What is the effect of the increased population of personified qualities (Beauty, Joy, Pleasure, Delight, Melancholy) in the last stanza?

Poe, "Sonnet—To Science"
Emerson, "Days"
Longfellow, "The Cross of Snow"
Arnold, "The Scholar-Gypsy": Compare the figure of "close-lipped patience" (line 194) with the "Patience" who speaks in Milton's "When I Consider How My Light Is Spent" (line 8). Should Arnold's "patience" be considered a proper instance of allegory or personification?
C. Rossetti, "Up-Hill"
Swinburne, "When the Hounds of Spring Are on Winter's Traces"
Yeats, "The Second Coming"
S. Crane, From *The Black Riders and Other Lines*
Larkin, "Sad Steps"
Rukeyser, "Ballad of Orange and Grape"
Rich, "Diving into the Wreck" *CD-ROM Link: Compare to the selections from Spenser's *Faerie Queene*: what devices do Rich and Spenser share in describing in considerable detail a difficult quest that is nonetheless clearly a spiritual one?
Momaday, "The Eagle-Feather Fan"
Wilner, "Reading the Bible Backwards"
Heaney, "The Skunk"
Komunyakaa, "Sunday Afternoons"
Muldoon, "Gathering Mushrooms"
Graham, "Opulence"
Dove, "Parsley" *CD-ROM Link
Lee, "Persimmons" *CD-ROM Link
Zarin, "The Ant Hill"

5.6 Conceit

As a kind of extended metaphor, or metaphor pushed to the absolute limit of detail (and beyond), the conceit is usually a trope that involves the entire poem; the very point is to demonstrate the poet's power to find all the unexpected and impossible likenesses in dissimilar objects and concepts. In this way, the conceit is to metaphor roughly what a fixed form such as the Petrarchan sonnet is to rhyme. An exercise: break your class into small groups and have each group diagram a conceit from a poem in the following selection. Have students identify the central metaphor/comparison pairing and then list all the ways in which the pair are likened. Which points of comparison are most startling or strange? Do they lead to a new perspective or insight—or do they simply seem strained and incredible?

Wyatt, "The Long Love, That in My Thought Doth Harbor": Compare with Surrey's handling of the same Petrarchan conceit in his translation. How have the points of comparison changed? What has been emphasized, de-emphasized?

Surrey, "Love, That Doth Reign and Live Within My Thought"
Spenser, From *Amoretti*
Donne, "The Flea"
Herbert, "The Altar"
Dickinson, #1763 ("Fame is a bee")
Dunbar, "Sympathy"
Frost, "The Silken Tent"
Stevens, "Peter Quince at the Clavier"
Clampitt, "Beethoven, Opus 111"
Erdrich, "Birth"

CHAPTER 6

Wordplay

Words—their sounds, their meanings, and the combinatorial effects of both—are the poet's medium. Few poems completely refuse the opportunity to make words perform in ways alien or unusual to their functions in ordinary discourse. Sometimes the effects may be a subtle weaving together of sound patterns that bind the atmospherics of a passage more tightly; sometimes the effects may be dazzling nonsense, calling the reader's attention forcibly to the words themselves as such. Often a poem mixes diction from heterogeneous discourses—placing latinate diction in the company of street slang or archaisms in the presence of the latest scientific terminology. Wordplay can be a poetics unto itself, as in **Stein's** *Stanzas in Meditation,* which reveals ways that words work on us by moving them out of their familiar roles, disrupting syntax, breaking down our comfortable assumption that words at their best must be translucent conductors of meaning. Most wordplay, however, is in the service of a particular task within the poem and may even pass unnoticed by the conscious thought of all but the most attuned reader. Getting your students in the habit of looking for wordplay and questioning its role in the poem's overall effect can open rich vistas in texts that seemed otherwise closed and inscrutable.

6.1 Words, Names, and Labels

Some poems reflect self-referentially on words as their medium. By ringing changes on two banal, clichéd adjectives ("nice" and "pretty"), **D. H. Lawrence** and **Stevie Smith** make them resonate with surprising meanings. **Carroll's** "Jabberwocky" invites speculation on how things get their names, on the power of words—that is, the power of mere combinations of sounds—to designate, label, and differentiate one thing from another. In "The Day Lady Died," **O'Hara's** day in New York City is largely a random accumulation of place-names, brand names, and titles. In what ways do these poems support, deny, or qualify the position that, as Robert Hass has put it, "a word is elegy to what it signifies"?

Blake, "The Lamb"
Carroll, "Jabberwocky"
Lawrence, "The English Are So Nice!"
Cummings, "my father moved through dooms of love"
S. Smith, "Pretty"
Lowry, "Strange Type"
Rukeyser, "Ballad of Orange and Grape"
O'Hara, "The Day Lady Died"
Corn, "Contemporary Culture and the Letter 'K' "
Palmer, "Fifth Prose"
Dove, "Parsley" *CD-ROM Link
Daniel Hall, "Mangosteens"
Lee, "Persimmons" *CD-ROM Link
Zarin, "The Ant Hill"

6.2 Sounds and Onomatopoeia

Related to the question of how things get their names, or of the relation of things to words, is the consideration of words as sounds, and poems as structures of sounds. Some poems insist more than others on the phonetics of poetry, or admit that just about all poetry can be produced in—or reduced to—the tongue, throat, and larynx. The question of whether words can sound like natural sounds, whether "rustle" makes a rustling sound, or "buzz" imitates the sound of bees, is much debated; students are often all too eager to detect such instances of onomatopoeia, and they are often surprised to learn that they are usually "hearing" sounds or qualities in the words only because of strong associations with the words' meanings. We find that students tend to attribute all sorts of qualities or feelings to the sounds of words that are clearly a property of the meaning of the words. An instructive trick: take a line such as "And evening full of the linnet's wings" and get the class to agree that the line produces a smooth, soothing, melodious sound from all its resonant en-in-ings, like the whirring wings it describes. Then alter the line to "A thieving fool for the sinner's winks": can you get the class to "hear" a "nasty, sneering, sniggering" sound in the line's resonance now? The following list includes poems whose sound is particularly prominent, usually through a combination of highly audible rhyme and strong rhythms (**Skelton, Hopkins**), and poems that invent nonsense words that make sense because of the associations of other words with similar sounds (**Carroll**), or that describe sounds (**Dryden, Merwin**).

Skelton, "To Mistress Margaret Hussey"
Dryden, "A Song for St. Cecilia's Day"
Poe, "The Raven"
Tennyson, "Break, Break, Break": It is surprising how readily students will claim to "hear" the sound of the crashing waves in this poem. To what degree is this an effect of the match of the rhythm of the poem and the rhythm of the sea-swells? To what degree is it a resemblance fostered by the meaning of the words, rather than their sound or rhythm? Revise the poem's opening to "Brook, brook, brook, / On thy smooth gray stones, O flow," and what does the repeated word "sound like"? (Or, more mischievously, "Brake, brake, brake / On thy coiled greased shocks, O Sedan . . . "). Compare imitative effects in "Dover Beach" (see "Versification").
Arnold, "Dover Beach"
Carroll, "Jabberwocky"
Hopkins, "The Windhover"
Stevens, "Of Mere Being"
Millay, "Euclid Alone Has Looked on Beauty Bare": Do we "hear [Beauty's] massive sandal set on stone" in the last line?
Moss, "Tourists"
Merwin, "The Drunk in the Furnace": A poem that describes a series of loud, grating sounds is a good place to investigate the question of whether the words that describe or name those sounds also echo or imitate them.
Heaney, "Casting and Gathering"
Graham, "Opulence"
Lee, "Persimmons" *CD-ROM Link

6.3 Diction

A. *Formal and Elevated Diction*

Formal, elaborate, strongly "poetic" language suggests ways in which poetry itself may be considered a kind of dialect, a branch of nonstandard

English. We have listed here a range of poems whose language is markedly "poetic," hieratic, or mannered in some way. Eighteenth-century poetry provides the most obvious examples, but the poetry of our own century has its own high styles as well. Often this high style is characterized by Latinate diction, allegorical or mythological figures, and grammatical inversions of normal word order. When would it be an insult, when a compliment, to call someone's speech or writing "poetic"? An exercise: rewrite in high poetic style a conversational phrase, a nursery rhyme, or a short colloquial poem. For a good example of how comic the results can be, see the section on "The Buskin Style" in Pope's *Peri Bathous*, where an everyday command, "Uncork the bottle and chip the bread," is preposterously inflated into "Apply thine engine to the spongy door, / Set Bacchus from his Glassy Prison free, / And strip white Ceres of her nut-brown Coat."

Lanyer, From *Salve Deus Rex Judaeorum*
Wilmot, "A Satire against Reason and Mankind"
Collins, "Ode on the Poetical Character"
Keats, "On First Looking into Chapman's Homer": Why does the diction become less heightened in the sonnet's sestet?
D. G. Rossetti, "The Blessed Damozel": How does Rossetti manage to establish a context of archaic words ("damozel," "herseemed") and phrasings ("And the stars in her hair were seven") so that even seemingly colloquial, straightforward usages ("yellow like ripe corn") take on a medieval aura or a taste of timeworn, obsolete English?
Hopkins, "[Thou Art Indeed Just, Lord . . .]"
Stevens, "Sunday Morning": To what degree is the heightened manner of this poem a matter of Latinate diction ("unsubdued elations," "ambiguous undulations") or a clash between Latinate and Anglo-Saxon words ("indifferent blue," "inarticulate pang"), or curious adjectives ("mythy")? To what degree does the poem's rhetoric—the long complex sentences, the frequent questions—contribute to the elevated manner? *CD-ROM Link
Lawrence, "Bavarian Gentians"
Hill, From *Mercian Hymns*

B. *Informal and Colloquial Diction*

This group of poems that feature everyday, conversational language is closely related to the topic of speaker (see secton 7.2, "Speakers, Characters, and Points of View"). To what degree are poems written in even the most simple, informal, or slangy diction and grammar marked by some "poetic" variant of the colloquial? See also the section on blank verse (section 1.2.B) for poems that attempt to reproduce or discover in iambic pentameter the everyday rhythms of English.

Skelton, "Mannerly Margery Milk and Ale": Which of the other poems on this list get as down-to-earth in their language as Skelton does in phrases such as, "I love you an whole cart-load" (line 9)?
Ralegh, "The Lie"
Donne, "The Canonization" and "Song ('Sweetest love, I do not go')": Just about all of the ingredients in "The Canonization" are simple words in common usage. Where then does its heightened poetic flavor come from?
Pope, "Epistle to Dr. Arbuthnot": Compare the blunt, imperative opening of this poem ("Shut, shut the door!") to the brusque first line of Donne's "The Canonization" ("For God's sake, hold your tongue . . . "). Which poem sustains that irritated, colloquial tone more consistently?
Wordsworth, "She Dwelt Among the Untrodden Ways" and "Resolution and Independence"
Whitman, "Song of Myself," section 24 ("Walt Whitman, a kosmos, of Manhattan the son"): How is Whitman's boast to be the medium of ordinary "dumb voices" undercut by his occasional use of heightened diction ("afflatus," line 50; "gambols," line 553) and poetically inverted word order ("the password primeval," line 506; "Voices indecent by me clarified," line 518)? Or are such elevated expressions counterbalanced by the blunt, unembarrassed inclusion of such words as "armpits" (line 525) and "dung" (line 515)? Does "dung" seem more polite when Swift uses it in "A Description of a City Shower" (line 61)?
Frost, "The Most of It"
Cummings, " 'next to of course god america i": Cummings enables us to hear a frightening strain of American talk: the inflated rhetoric of knee-jerk patriotism sounds even emptier beside the self-congratulatory, complacent slang. What is the effect of the snatches of songs mixed in with such vernacular expressions as those piled up in line 8? How does the poem's last line underscore the phony theatricality of the orator's performance?

C. *Abstract vs. Concrete Diction*

That abstract diction consists of words referring to intangible concepts, and concrete diction of words referring to tangible objects, is a distinction quickly taught. As an exercise, have your students find examples of concrete and abstract diction in several poems. It is important for them to see that just as formal and informal diction can mixed, so too can be abstract and concrete diction. Also, the formal vs. informal distinction needs to be drawn apart from the abstract vs. concrete distinction. For instance, a poem can be formal and abstract, as in **Shakespeare's** Sonnet 116, or formal and concrete, as in **Hopkins's** "Pied Beauty."

Shakespeare, Sonnet 116 ("Let me not to the marriage of true minds")
Dickinson, #709 ("Publication—is the Auction")
Hopkins, "Pied Beauty"
Stevens, "Sunday Morning" *CD-ROM Link: This poem mixes a wealth of concrete and abstract diction. How do they function together? How do the abstract phrases illuminate the meaning of the concrete images and vice versa?
Moore, "The Fish" and "What Are Years?": These two poems have somewhat similar themes, both endorsing a thriving stoicism. Both also display Moore's gift for intricate stanza patterns, and both employ generally formal diction—yet the diction of the former is almost entirely concrete, that of the latter abstract. Is the loss in clarity of image outweighed by the (apparent) gain in clarity of rhetoric?
Donald Hall, "Prophecy"
Erdrich, "I Was Sleeping Where the Black Oaks Move"
Zarin, "Song"

6.4 Light Verse

Which of these poems could be labeled nonsense verse, or poetry for children, and which would be funny only to adults? In discussing what makes these poems amusing, it is good to remember that the particular techniques alone cannot be called comic, as writers of light verse use a number of devices to comic effect that are not necessarily funny in other contexts (outlandish rhymes, invented words, surprise endings).

Lyly, "Oh, For a Bowl of Fat Canary"
Donne, "The Flea": With its seductive cleverness and humorous (or alarming?) intensity, could this poem count as adult light verse? Compare its tone to that of Byron's *Don Juan* and Hecht's "The Ghost in the Martini."
Gray, "Ode (On the Death of a Favorite Cat, Drowned in a Tub of Goldfishes)"
Byron, From *Don Juan,* both the Fragment on the Back of the Ms. of Canto I and Canto the First
Lear, "The Owl and the Pussy-Cat" and "How Pleasant to Know Mr. Lear"
Carroll, "Jabberwocky"

Gilbert, "I Am the Very Model of a Modern Major-General" and "Titwillow"
Hardy, "The Ruined Maid"
Parker, "Résumé" and "One Perfect Rose"
Brown, "Slim in Atlanta": Given its strong satirical edge, can this humorous mockery of the perils of a racially segregated society count as light verse?
Nash, "Reflections on Ice-breaking"
S. Smith, "Mr. Over"
Hecht, "The Ghost in the Martini"
Merrill, "The Victor Dog": What gives this energetically playful poem an earnestness or allegorical tone that may suggest it is a rather more ambitious kind of light verse than other poems on this list?
Mathews, "Histoire"

CHAPTER 7

Rhetoric

7.1 Audience, Address, and Apostrophe

Various modes of address, often marked by the device of apostrophe, are a traditional and central device in some poetic genres. Most odes will include some moments in which the subject of the ode is directly addressed or invoked: the breathless "Thou"s and "Oh"s of the Romantic ode can seem to make apostrophizing hard work. Elegies, too, conventionally speak to the dead person, and often as well use apostrophe in calling upon other people, or mythological creatures, for consolation. Epics begin by apostrophizing or invoking the muse, and apostrophes may call upon some animating spirit to enter the poet or to come to him or her. This list attempts to illustrate the variety of things poets will apostrophize—the muse, a rose, the sea, the wind. (See section 3.1, "Titles," for a listing of poems that are titled *to* someone or something.)

Apostrophe can be problematic when we try to imagine poems as the utterances of hypothetical speakers (see section 7.2, "Speakers, Characters, and Points of View"), since it is hard to imagine in just what circumstances, outside of a poem, a speaker would talk directly to a lute, a nightingale, a rose, the wind, etc. This problem also raises the issue of the poem's intended audience: for whom was the poem written? Sometimes audience is defined by occasion (see section 7.1.A, "Occasional Poetry"), but more often poetry seems to address no exact audience. John Stuart

Mill claimed that this was because poetry was distinct from rhetoric: "Rhetoric is heard; poetry is overheard." But a text must be rhetorical if it has been deliberately constructed—by the use of apostrophes to inanimate objects or abstract concepts, for instance—so that any reader is likely to feel as if she or he were eavesdropping. The very trick of creating an indirect form of address that seems aimed at no one reader or group of readers is itself part of a rhetoric of universality: the poem pretends to speak not as a part of a localized, historical discourse but to the invisible audience of the ages. Of course, not all poems participate in this rhetoric, and many poems address both a particular and a general readership.

Anonymous, "The Cuckoo Song"

Chaucer, "Complaint to His Purse" and "To His Scribe Adam"

Anonymous, "Western Wind": Compare this tiny lyric to Shelley's grand "Ode to the West Wind." How is the relationship of apostrophizer to apostrophized different in the two poems despite the fact that both address the west wind?

Skelton, "To Mistress Margaret Hussey"

Anonymous, "Weep You No More, Sad Fountains": What is the effect of the shift from "sad fountains" to "sad eyes" as the object of the apostrophe? Compare Jonson's "Slow, Slow, Fresh Fount."

Wyatt, "My Lute Awake!": How is the apostrophe to the lute almost like an apostrophe to the poem itself as it proceeds?

Queen Elizabeth I, "[Ah silly pugg wert thou so sore afraid]": This is a rarity in English—a poem written by a monarch to one of her subjects, in this case Elizabeth's favorite courtier, Sir Walter Ralegh. The poem's address is direct and intimate: is there any hint at all that this text, originally circulated privately in manuscript, is addressed to larger audience? What might that audience be?

Drayton, "To the Reader of these Sonnets": How is direct address to the invisible and characterless "reader" just as artificial as an apostrophe to a lute, a god, or a force of nature? Compare with Jonson's epigram "To the Reader."

Marlowe, "The Passionate Shepherd to His Love" *CD-ROM Link: Given that the title indicates an intimate and closed address, is this poetry simply "overheard," as Mill would have it? And if the poem is not addressed only by a shepherd to his love, to whom is it addressed? You might help your students with this question by reading also Ralegh's "The Nymph's Reply to the Shepherd." This is a good opportunity to introduce the concept of coterie verse by pointing out that, in Elizabethan courtly circles, poems were seen as an accomplishment of gentility and were passed hand-to-hand in manuscript form. (See also the above questions on Elizabeth's own specimen, "[Ah silly pugg wert thou so sore afraid].") Only later were the poems collected and printed for the edification of the emerging literate middle class in the form of anthologies such as *Tottel's Miscellany*. What does this origin tell us about how the rhetoric of these poems differs from that of our contemporary poetry, which generally presumes a silent, anonymous readership of printed texts.

Shakespeare, "Blow, Blow, Thou Winter Wind"

Donne, "The Sun Rising"

Herbert, "Virtue"

Waller, "Song ('Go, lovely rose!')"

Milton, "L'Allegro" and "Il Penseroso": Why do these poems begin with apostrophes to a caricatured, extreme, allegorical version of the state of mind they wish to banish?

Lovelace, "The Grasshopper"

Vaughan, "They Are All Gone into the World of Light!": The opening meditation on departed friends might lead us to expect that the poet would invoke those friends; why do we instead get apostrophes to "holy hope, and high humility" (line 13), "Dear, beauteous death" (line 17), and "Father of eternal life" (line 33)?

Gray, "Ode (On the Death of a Favorite Cat, Drowned in a Tub of Goldfishes)"

Byron, "On This Day I Complete My Thirty-sixth Year": What is the function of the self-correction or self-clarification of who or what is being commanded to "Awake!" in lines 25–26?

Shelley, "Ode to the West Wind"

Tennyson, "Break, Break, Break"

Whitman, "Crossing Brooklyn Ferry"

Arnold, "The Scholar-Gypsy": This poem begins with an apostrophe to the long-deceased Scholar-Gypsy, and almost seems to create his ghostly presence by repeatedly addressing him. But matters get particularly interesting later in the poem: why does the speaker invoke the Scholar-Gypsy only to warn him to keep away from the invoker and "this strange disease of modern life" (line 203)?

Dickinson, #249 ("Wild Nights—Wild Nights!"): All of Dickinson's poems raise intriguing questions about audience. No specific audience is named, although we know that she showed some of her poems to female family members and, through correspondence, to the editor of *The Atlantic Monthly*. Yet she made little effort to publish her poems during her lifetime and left instructions for their destruction after her death. For and to whom, then, was she writing?

Yeats, "Sailing to Byzantium": What is the effect of delaying the apostrophe of the "sages" until the third stanza?

Stevens, "The Idea of Order at Key West": Why does the speaker address "Ramon Fernandez," in line 44?

Jeffers, "Shine, Perishing Republic": Compare the final address to "boys" (line 9) with the advice addressed to "ye beauties" in the last stanza of Gray's "Ode (On the Death of a Favorite Cat, Drowned in a Tub of Goldfishes)"
Moore, "Nevertheless"
Eliot, "The Dry Salvages": How can we account for the endurance of the musty old device of apostrophe, even into high modernism? What is the effect of the apostrophe in lines 162ff.?
Snodgrass, "Mementos"
Sissman, From "Dying: An Introduction," "IV. Path. Report"

A. *Occasional Poetry*

Although this is a large topic, it can be useful at the beginning of a poetry survey. Students coming to their first college course on poetry may be asking, Why do poets write poems at all? Does a poet need a reason to write a poem? What sorts of things happening in the world at large can be a sufficient goad to get a poem started? Rather than treat what is conventionally termed "occasional poetry" (verse commissioned for, or written to commemorate, a public event such as a coronation, holiday, anniversary) as a separate mode, we prefer to introduce it as a specific answer to a large question about the range of stimuli that may spark a poem into being written. It is important for beginning students to learn that poems can be occasioned by events as dissimilar in nature and scope as the sight of a rainbow and the advent of a season, the death of a pet rabbit and the massacre of a huge number of people. (Elegies could be fruitfully included in this topic.) The urge to write a poem is as varied as the impetus behind any kind of utterance; to celebrate something, to console oneself, to pray, to commemorate, to praise. Or a poet may write to correct what he or she sees as errors in earlier poems, or to register pleasure in the act of poetry-making itself. It is not always easy to distinguish between a poem's occasion and what we more simply call its subject or topic of concern, but here we have isolated poems that announce themselves as responses to some quite specific occasion, including the special sense of holiday or marked day on the calendar. Nor is it always easy to distinguish between a poem's real occasion and the fictions it suggests of that occasion.

Poems on Personal Occasions

Askew, "The Ballad Which Anne Askewe Made and Sang When She Was in Newgate"
Bradstreet, "Before the Birth of One of Her Children" and "Here Follows Some Verses Upon the Burning of Our House July 10th, 1666"

Philips, "To My Excellent Lucasia, on Our Friendship"
Wordsworth, "Composed upon Westminster Bridge, September 3, 1802"
Byron, "On This Day I Complete My Thirty-sixth Year"
Arnold, "To Marguerite"
Dickinson, #49 ("I never lost as much but twice"): Here the actual occasion that prompts the poem is quite uncertain; we know only that it is occasioned by a terrible, unspecified loss. Does this open or close the poem's address to us as readers?
Williams, "This Is Just to Say" *CD-ROM Link
Larkin, "Church Going" and "For Sidney Bechet"
Porter, "An Exequy"
Heaney, "Casting and Gathering"
Ondaatje, From "Rock Bottom," "(Ends of the Earth)"
Zarin, "Song"

POEMS ON PUBLIC OCCASIONS

Milton, "On the Morning of Christ's Nativity" and "On the Late Massacre in Piedmont"
Dryden, "A Song for St. Cecilia's Day"
Emerson, "Concord Hymn": Why does Emerson mention that the famous bridge on this site is no longer there? In what sense will the newly completed monument replace the ruined bridge? (This poem has been inscribed on the Concord Monument). An exercise: in conjunction with the poems in this group, and Emerson's in particular, ask students to look for and copy down commemorative inscriptions on buildings or monuments. Compare how these local inscriptions take up the task of marking a commemorative occasion and marking the building or structure as a site for commemoration.
Howe, "Battle-Hymn of the Republic"
Hardy, "The Convergence of the Twain": To illustrate the wide range of possible poetic occasions, compare Hardy's poem on a monumental, tragic, and public convergence with Frost's miniature drama of convergence, "Design."
Yeats, "Easter 1916" *CD-ROM Link
MacDiarmid, From "In Memoriam James Joyce"

7.2 Speakers, Characters, and Points of View

The fiction that in a poem we hear a voice speaking is one of its most persistent and powerful devices. This list illustrates the range of voices that a poem may invent, not all of them human. For convenience in an introductory course, the poems listed here are all in the first person, but it is arguable that all poems fictionalize or create figures of voice.

Beowulf

Anonymous, Riddles, 1 ("I am a lonely being, scarred by swords"): How does the use of first person create a point of view for an object? Is this reverse apostrophe—the object talks back?

Anonymous, "The Seafarer"

Chaucer, "The Pardoner's Prologue and Tale" *CD-ROM Link

Anonymous, "Tom o' Bedlam's Song"

Tichborne, "Tichborne's Elegy": As an exercise, have students read this poem from a handout or projection that does not include the italicized line above the first line or the historical footnote. Without any knowledge of the poet's historical circumstances, does this poem make any sense? How do the students characterize the speaker before reading the note? After?

Donne, "The Relic"

Jonson, "Though I Am Young and Cannot Tell"

Herbert, "Affliction (I)" and "The Collar": How does the past-tense, first-person narration in "The Collar" change our point of view?

Blake, "The Little Black Boy"

Burns, "Holy Willie's Prayer"

Wordsworth, "Lines Composed a Few Miles Above Tintern Abbey": The speaker of this poem seems much closer to the poet, the historical Wordsworth, than the speaker of Blake's "The Little Black Boy" seems to Blake, or that of Plath's "Elm" seems to Plath; nonetheless, what means do all these poems share to create the fiction of a voice speaking the poem?

Clare, "I Am": Compare to Thoreau's, "I Am a Parcel of Vain Strivings Tied"

R. Browning, "My Last Duchess"

Whitman, "Song of Myself" *CD-ROM Link

Mew, "The Farmer's Bride"

MacDiarmid, From "In Memoriam James Joyce"

S. Smith, "Not Waving but Drowning": This poem contains a speaker within a speaker and is all about the ironies of perspective: whose perspective differs from whose and with what results? Where are we as readers in this tableau and who is talking to us?

Bishop, "One Art": How does this villanelle, despite the rigors of its fixed form, manage to breathe life into the fiction that we are overhearing the speaker talking to herself during the actual process of writing the poem? What effects does the poem gain by this trick? How, then, is this "overheard" lyric also a piece of public rhetoric?

O'Hara, "Why I Am Not a Painter": Compare O'Hara's way of using the first person to convey the distinction between poets and painters with Ashbery's third-person depiction of a painter in/as a poem in "The Painter."
Plath, "Lady Lazarus"
Lorde, "Coal"
Raine, "A Martian Sends a Postcard Home"
Soto, "Not Knowing"
Leithauser, "In Minako Wada's House"
Duffy, "Warming Her Pearls"
Lee, "Persimmons" *CD-ROM Link

A. *Tone*

Tone has to do with the attitude the speaker takes toward his or her own words, an attitude we as readers may or may not share, or that the poet who invented the speaker may or may not share. For which of these poems is the tone established right from the first line, for which does it take the reader somewhat longer to determine the most likely tone of the poem as a whole, and in which does the tone change as the poem progresses? How does the range of available or acceptable tones or speaking attitudes widen in the twentieth century?

Chaucer, "Complaint to His Purse"
Blake, "Holy Thursday [II.]"
Byron, "Written After Swimming from Sestos to Abydos"
Meredith, *Modern Love*, 17 ("At dinner, she is hostess, I am host")
Dickinson, #216 ("Safe in their Alabaster Chambers—"): Compare the 1859 and 1861 versions. How does the revised second stanza alter the tone of the whole poem?
C. Rosetti, "Song ('When I am dead, my dearest')"
Hardy, "Channel Firing"
Pound, "The Seafarer": Compare the tone of Pound's free translation/re-creation with that of Hamer's stricter translation of "The Seafarer" in this volume. What aspects of the speaker's attitude does Pound play up or even exaggerate? What religious comfort does he deny the poem by not translating the final thirty-five lines, and how does this also change the tone?
Corso, "Marriage"
Baraka, "An Agony. As Now."
Fenton, "In Paris with You"

7.3 Monologue

Whenever a poem maintains the fiction of a stable, single speaker, whether that speaker is anonymous or identified with the poet or identified with a particular historical or fictional character, that poem is a monologue. Monologues are not monolithic, however: they range from the expressive "cry of the heart" of "Western Wind" to the ironic narrative recollection of **Cullen's** "Incident" to the long meditation of **Wordsworth's** "Lines Composed a Few Miles Above Tintern Abbey" to the dramatic and satiric character portrait of **R. Browning's** "The Bishop Orders His Tomb at Saint Praxed's Church." Since monologue poems offer a variety of speakers, many poems that could be listed in this section are listed in section 7.2 above and vice versa. Probably the two sections should be taught together.

A. *Dramatic Monologue*

This is a specialized genre. The designation "dramatic monologue" can be a bit misleading, as the speaker of these poems does not, as a rule, soliloquize on a bare stage. The speaker of a dramatic monologue generally has a listener. Furthermore, unlike speakers in poetry generally, the fictive speaker of the dramatic monologue is identifiable as an individual and usually maintains the fiction of actual, credible speech, rather than merely maintaining a first-person perspective in a text otherwise utterly unlike conversational language. In which poems does the speaker's continuing to talk seem to depend most heavily on the listener's lending an ear? Which poems use the speaker's own words to reveal unflattering or ironic aspects of character?

Chaucer, "The Prologue" from "The Pardoner's Prologue and Tale" *CD-ROM Link: Because it is part a larger poem of heterogeneous narrative verse, this passage is not generally conceived of as a dramatic monologue, but taken in isolation it shares many of the features of the much later poems by R. Browning that were composed to stand alone.

Marlowe, "The Passionate Shepherd to His Love" *CD-ROM Link

Landor, "Dying Speech of an Old Philosopher": This dramatic monologue reads more like a carefully composed soliloquy. Is the fictional situation and characterization suggested by the title necessary to our understanding of the poem? An exercise: have your class read the poem from handouts or a projection without showing them the title. Ask them to characterize the speaker and situation, then show them the title and discuss the difference between it and their hypotheses. Then compare this poem to a Browning poem, such as "The Bishop

Orders His Tomb at Saint Praxed's Church"—how is the "Bishop" more precise a character than Landor's "Philosopher," even though both are fictions?

Tennyson, "Ulysses" *CD-ROM Link and "Tithonus": Compare the character of Ulysses to the title character of "The Seafarer." How do they differ in tone and outlook? Would you call "The Seafarer" a dramatic monologue?

R. Browning, "My Last Duchess," "The Bishop Orders His Tomb at Saint Praxed's Church," and "Fra Lippo Lippi"

Hardy, "Channel Firing"

Housman, "Is My Team Ploughing"

Yeats, "Crazy Jane Talks with the Bishop"

Pound, "The River-Merchant's Wife: a Letter"

L. Hughes, "The Negro Speaks of Rivers"

Berryman, From "Homage to Mistress Bradstreet"

Judith Wright, "Eve to Her Daughters"

Brooks,"We Real Cool" *CD-ROM Link: Not a dramatic monologue, strictly speaking, but the use of the first-person plural gives voice to a fictionalized collective character, that of the doomed young men whose slang the poem borrows and hones to a tragic edge.

Glück, "Gretel in Darkness"

B. *Meditation, Confession, and Invitation*

These categories of monologue have become the dominant rhetorical form of poetry in English during the past two centuries. For that reason only a tiny fraction of the possible listings is represented here. It might be useful to contrast some of these poems with those in the category of dramatic monologue above, and once again to raise the question of audience (see section 7.1.A) for such apparently private compositions.

Queen Elizabeth I, "[The doubt of future foes exiles my present joy]"

Shakespeare, Sonnet 29 ("When, in disgrace with fortune and men's eyes")

Donne, Holy Sonnet 5 ("I am a little world made cunningly")

Jonson, "To Penshurst"

Herbert, "The Collar" and "The Pulley": Compare the latter with Taylor's "Meditation 8," listed below. Both poems end in startling tropes based on the Christian communion ritual and figuring God's love as an act of consumption—" 'You must sit down,' says Love, 'and taste my meat.' / So I did sit and eat"; "Eat, eat me, soul, and thou shalt never die." How can such apparently bizarre dialogue emerge out of the very nature of deep devotional meditation, which we tend to think of as a kind of monologue?

Milton, "When I Consider How My Light Is Spent"
Bradstreet, "Before the Birth of One of Her Children"
Taylor, "Meditation 8 ('I kenning through astronomy divine')"
Gray, "Elegy Written in a Country Churchyard": One of the most famous examples of the outdoor meditation, this poem presents itself as having been composed or even written while its author was out walking through village, countryside, or wilderness. The convention thrives to the present day—see, for instance, Ammons's "Corsons Inlet" or Snyder's "Above Pate Valley."
Cowper, "Lines Written During a Period of Insanity"
Wordsworth, "Lines Composed a Few Miles Above Tintern Abbey": This poem is not generally labeled a dramatic monologue, but in the context of the Tennyson and Browning selections listed in secton 7.3.A above, the discovery around line 114 that the speaker's sister accompanies him can begin to change our sense of the speaker's meditative isolation.
Coleridge, "Frost at Midnight"
Byron, "On This Day I Complete My Thirty-sixth Year"
Shelley, "Stanzas Written in Dejection, Near Naples"
Keats, "Ode to a Nightingale" and "Ode on Melancholy"; also, "When I Have Fears" and "This Living Hand" can be taught in tandem.
Tennyson, From "In Memoriam A. H. H.," 119 ("Doors, where my heart was used to beat")
R. Browning, "Home-Thoughts, From Abroad"
Thoreau, "I Am a Parcel of Vain Strivings Tied"
Whitman, "Vigil Strange I Kept on the Field One Night"
Arnold, "Dover Beach"
Dickinson, #613 ("They shut me up in Prose—")
Hardy, "I Look into My Glass"
Hopkins, "[No Worst, There Is None. Pitched Past Pitch of Grief]"
Yeats, "The Lake Isle of Innisfree" and "Lapis Lazuli"
Frost, "Birches" and "Acquainted with the Night"
Stein, From *Stanzas in Meditation*: How is it that these stanzas can be called meditative?
Stevens, "The Idea of Order at Key West"
Lawrence, "Piano"
Moore, "What Are Years?"
Millay, "I, Being Born a Woman and Distressed"
Owen, "Dulce Et Decorum Est" *CD-ROM Link
Cummings, "my father moved through dooms of love"
Auden, "As I Walked Out One Evening"
Roethke, "The Lost Son"
Bishop, "The Moose"
Hayden, "Those Winter Sundays"

Berryman, Dream Song 14 ("Life, friends, is boring. We must not say so")
D. Thomas, "Fern Hill" *CD-ROM Link
R. Lowell, "My Last Afternoon with Uncle Devereux Winslow"
Larkin, "Talking in Bed"
Kinnell, "After Making Love We Hear Footsteps"
Plath, "Daddy"
Harrison, "A Kumquat for John Keats"
Heaney, "Digging"
Erdrich, "I Was Sleeping Where the Black Oaks Move"
Zarin, "The Ant Hill"

C. *Letters*

Poems that take the form of letters addressed from one person to another raise in direct and easily grasped terms the way a poem may be a circuit of communication. Since the poem must on some level also be addressed to us, as readers, we can compare the ways that these poems serve the needs of both private and public audiences. How is reading poems like reading someone else's mail, with the accompanying thrills and hazards of overhearing a communication not addressed to us?

Bradstreet, "A Letter to Her Husband, Absent upon Public Employment"
Pope, "Epistle to Miss Blount" and "Epistle to Dr. Arbuthnot"
Leapor, "The Epistle of Deborah Dough"
Williams, "This Is Just to Say" *CD-ROM Link
Pound, "The River-Merchant's Wife: a Letter"
Van Duyn, "Letters from a Father"
Kinnell, "The Correspondence School Instructor Says Goodbye to His Poetry Students"
James Wright, "A Note Left in Jimmy Leonard's Shack"
Raine, "A Martian Sends a Postcard Home"

7.4 Dialogue

Poems structured around the exchange of two or more speakers may illustrate a range of rhetorical effects: the dialogue may be an outright debate or argument (as in **P. Sidney's** "Ye Goatherd Gods") or a static pair of statements of each speaker's position on a matter about which they are too opposed even to debate (**Blake, Ransom**). In some poems one speaker seems to act as straight man setting up the other's punchlines, or as a mere interlocutor giving the main speaker an opportunity to hold forth (**Pope, Yeats, Frost**); in other poems, one speaker asks questions and another gives answers (**Rossetti, Housman**). These poems may serve to introduce such forms as the ode, in which one stanza may respond to another in a muted or implied dialogue (**Wordsworth,** "Ode: Intimations of Immortality"), or the sonnet, many of which might be taught as a dialogue of alternate voices or points of view (**Shakespeare,** Sonnet 65). A consideration of which voice tends to get the last word in poetic dialogues (or in odes and sonnets) links this schematic grouping to the topic of closure (see section 3.4, "Closure").

Early Modern Ballads: "Lord Randal" and "The Unquiet Grave"
Sidney, "Ye Goatherd Gods"
Herbert, "Love (III)"
Pope, "Epistle to Dr. Arbuthnot"
Gay, Songs from *The Beggar's Opera*, "Air XVI"
Blake, "The Clod & the Pebble": Compare to other dialogues about love and to Herbert's "Love (III)." On the topic of love, which speaker in these poems might be said to take the part of clod (love is selfless and uplifting) and which of pebble (love is selfish, envious, and demeaning)?
C. Rossetti, "Up-Hill"
Hardy, "The Ruined Maid"
Housman, "Is My Team Ploughing"
Edward Thomas, "As the team's head brass"
Sassoon, " 'They' "
Ransom, "Piazza Piece"
Merrill, From *The Book of Ephraim*
O'Hara, "Why I Am Not a Painter"
Hass, "Tahoe in August"

7.5 Cited or Interpolated Voices

A number of poems include as a central fiction the words of another voice. Some of these poems may be best taught in conjunction with poems that stage a dialogue, or with poems that are framed by an introductory setting or are told as tales-within-a-tale (see section 3.5, "Framing Devices"). It may be useful to try to distinguish between poems in which this second voice seems to interpose itself willfully and those in which it is invited into the poem.

Milton, "Lycidas": What is the function of the series of voices, heard from one or many lines (Phoebus, Neptune, Camus, St. Peter)? See also Milton's "When I Consider How My Light Is Spent," where the voice of "Patience" completes the poem.
Coleridge, "The Rime of the Ancient Mariner": How many different

voices do we hear in this poem? Should we distinguish the voice of the narrator from the voice of the marginal annotations? In what ways does the dialogue between the First Voice and the Second Voice at the beginning of Part VI resemble the reader's voice questioning the poem and the poem (or the narrator?) replying?

D. G. Rossetti, "The Blessed Damozel": Are the voice of the speaker, the voice of the Blessed Damozel, and the voice who speaks inside parentheses best read as three separate voices?

Whitman, "Out of the Cradle Endlessly Rocking": What is the relation between the voice of the bird and the voice that speaks the poem? between both and the voice of the sea?

Eliot, *The Waste Land*: The poem is a veritable choir of many different voices, quoted, invented, ventriloquized. One way of teaching the poem is to investigate the varieties and development of these voices, from the Dantean words of the poem's dedication to the voice of Tiresias (lines 215ff.), from the barroom Cockney of lines 139–72 (ending with lines of Ophelia) to the voice of the thunder speaking words from the Upanishads.

Hayden, "Night, Death, Mississippi"
Hecht, "The Ghost in the Martini"
Strand, "Always"
Heaney, "Casting and Gathering"
Dove, "Parsley" *CD-ROM Link
Daniel Hall, "Mangosteens"
Erdrich, "I Was Sleeping Where the Black Oaks Move"
Lee, "Persimmons" *CD-ROM Link

7.6 Questions, Epiphanies, and Exhortations

Poems that ask questions, or are occasioned by a question, generally set out to do more than provide answers. This topic may be usefully linked to apostrophe (see section 7.1), since often the poet asks a question directly of the subject that she or he addresses. When a question recurs in a refrain, how may the intervening stanzas, by refusing or delaying an answer, lend it an added urgency? Why are love poems (**Sidney, Donne**) so often structured upon a series of questions? How does the centrality of questions in both love poetry and religious poetry suggest deeper affinities between these topics?

Anonymous, "Western Wind"
Anonymous, "Lord Randal"
Sidney, From *Astrophel and Stella*, 31 ("With how sad steps, Oh Moon, thou climb'st the skies")

Shakespeare, Sonnet 146 ("Poor soul, the center of my sinful earth") *CD-ROM Link
Donne, "Woman's Constancy"
Herbert, "Jordan (I)"
Carew, "A Song ('Ask me no more where Jove bestows')": How does the speaker's repeated refusal to be questioned act as a substitute for a question?
Suckling, "Song ('Why so pale and wan, fond lover?')"
Montagu, "A Receipt to Cure the Vapors"
Blake, "The Lamb" and "The Tyger"
Shelley, "Ode to the West Wind": What is the effect of a question coming at the end of a poem that is characterized throughout by exclamations and imperatives? Compare to the shifts from exclamations to questions and back again in Shelley's "To a Skylark."
Keats, "Ode on a Grecian Urn" and "Ode to a Nightingale": What larger differences between these two odes are suggested when we note that "Urn" moves through a series of questions to end with an epigrammatic pronouncement, while "Nightingale" moves through exclamations and pronouncements ("Already with thee!") to end with a question? Compare the questions in "To Autumn"—do that ode's questions seem easier to answer, or less in need of an answer?
Emerson, "The Rhodora": What besides the subtitle, "On being asked, whence is the flower?", suggests that this poem is an answer to a question? Compare the method and range of Emerson's answer to "whence is the flower?" to Whitman's answer to "What is the grass?" in "Song of Myself" (section 6). Is "whence" a narrower question than "what"?
E. B. Browning, *Sonnets from the Portuguese*, 43 ("How do I love thee? Let me count the ways")
Poe, "Sonnet—To Science"
Whitman, "Song of Myself," 6 ("A child said *What is the grass?* fetching it to me with full hands"): Why doesn't Whitman use Blake's method and ask the question directly of the grass itself ("Oh, grass, what are you?")? Compare with Sandburg's, "Grass," where the grass is the speaker.
S. Crane, From *The Black Riders and Other Lines* (XXV)
Frost, "Design"
Rukeyser, "Ballad of Orange and Grape"
Wilbur, "Advice to a Prophet"
Corso, "Marriage"
Baraka, "In Memory of Radio"
Muldoon, "Gathering Mushrooms"
Zarin, "Song"

II. Traditions and Counter-Traditions

CHAPTER 8

Myth and History

8.1 Allusion

Allusion is difficult for students to appreciate, particularly as it usually involves references with which they are not personally familiar. We recommend introducing the subject via contemporary references, especially the lyrics of popular songs, which often allude to current celebrities and events. The point is first to demystify allusion, stripping away the assumption that it is necessarily reference to ancient (and, to students, arcane) knowledge, and then to get students to see its value to poets. Allusion allows the poet to compact description and clarify connotation: a reference to a story, person, event, or text can save both poet and reader periphrastic explanations. Even if the allusion has first to be learned, its value to the poem becomes apparent on subsequent readings, once one knows the shorthand. Allusion is often used as a kind of trope as well, and it is as valuable a tool of comparison as metaphor and of substitution as metonymy.

A. A *Selection of Highly Allusive Poems*

Anonymous, "Now Go'th Sun Under Wood"
Dunbar, "In Prais of Wemen"
Anonymous, "Tom o' Bedlam's Song"

Shakespeare, "The Phoenix and the Turtle"
Lanyer, From *Salve Deus Rex Judeaorum*
Milton, "Lycidas" and *Paradise Lost,* Book 1
Pope, "The Rape of the Lock"
Johnson, "The Vanity of Human Wishes"
Barbauld, "The Rights of Woman" *CD-ROM Link
Landor, "Past Ruined Ilion Helen Lives"
Shelley, "Adonais"
Keats, "On First Looking into Chapman's Homer"
Tennyson, "The Lady of Shalott"
R. Browning, "Fra Lippo Lippi"
Melville, "The Portent"
Yeats, "Among School Children"
Stevens, "Peter Quince at the Clavier"
Pound, "Hugh Selwyn Mauberly: Life and Contacts"
Moore, "The Mind Is an Enchanting Thing"
Eliot, "The Love Song of J. Alfred Prufrock" and "Sweeney Among the Nightingales"
Graves, "The White Goddess"
L. Hughes, "The Negro Speaks of Rivers"
Auden, "Musée des Beaux Arts"
Jarrell, "A Man Meets a Woman in the Street"
Judith Wright, "Eve to Her Daughters"
R. Lowell, "Mr. Edwards and the Spider"
Clampitt, "Beethoven, Opus 111"
Larkin, "MCMXIV"
Hecht, " 'More Light! More Light!' "
Creeley, "Bresson's Movies"
Merrill, From *The Book of Ephraim*
Donald Hall, From "The One Day," "Prophecy"
Harrison, "A Kumquat for John Keats"
Hass, "Tahoe in August"
Corn, "Contemporary Culture and the Letter 'K' "
Glück, "Gretel in Darkness"
Fenton, "Dead Soldiers"
Christopher, "The Palm Reader"
Daniel Hall, "Mangosteens"
Schnackenberg, "Darwin in 1881"
Zarin, "Song"

B. Allusive Pairings

Dickinson, #1545 ("The Bible is an antique volume—") and Watts, "Our God, Our Help": On some level all of Dickinson's poems may be considered allusions to—and revisions, if not parodies, of—the neat, faithful hymns of Watts, among others. Rejecting the unquestioning pieties of Watts, Dickinson twists his meter, which had been regular to make it singable by a congregation. What changes would have to be made to the Watts poem to make it into a Dickinson poem?

Housman, "Is My Team Ploughing" and Early Modern Ballads: Which ballads is Housman's updated version responding to most closely? Compare Housman's updating of the ballad with Auden's in "As I Walked Out One Evening."

Eliot, *The Waste Land*: A pervasively and deeply allusive poem; what sorts of demands does such erudite poetry place upon the reader? Which of Eliot's own footnotes to the poem are seriously useful references, and which are jokes upon learned annotations?

Auden, "As I Walked Out One Evening" and Early Modern Ballads

Levertov, "O Taste and See" and Wordsworth, "The World Is Too Much with Us"

8.2 Mythology

Mythological references represent a special kind of allusion. They begin at least as sacred lore and become "mythology" in poems written by nonbelievers or would-be believers, who borrow the references to illustrate an alien or altered worldview from the one that generated the myths in the first place. Mythological reference that springs directly from a living system of belief cannot be called mythological without risk of offending the believer, and sacred references are used differently than allusions to elements of bygone or alien beliefs. Ask your students to look for the difference between mythology alluded to for convenience and mythology alluded to in reverence. A good starting point might be a comparison of Donne's Holy Sonnet 14 ("Batter my heart, three-personed God; for You") or Herbert's "Jordan (I)" with Larkin's "Church Going."

A. *Western Classical Mythology*

This group includes poems that mourn the passing of "a creed outworn" (**Wordsworth, Poe**) and poems that debunk the old myths as "an overheated farmhand's literature" (**Walcott**) or as a perpetuation of outmoded or oppressive ways of thinking. But whether wistful or scornful or simply opportunistic, these are the mythological references of poets for whom the classical deities are not living gods but a treasury of archaic allusions, useful or not. Notice, however, that allusions to dead beliefs often intermingle freely with living, even contentious religious devotion.

P. Sidney, "What Length of Verse?"

Jonson, "A Fit of Rhyme Against Rhyme" and "A Sonnet to the Noble Lady, the Lady Mary Wroth"

Milton, "On the Morning of Christ's Nativity": The birth of the Christ child routs all the pagan deities, scattering them from the woods and altars they inhabited. The nymphs and dryads of classical mythology are banished, it seems, to poetry itself; thus Milton can compare the infant Christ with the infant Hercules, who strangled a snake in his cradle. Ironically, celebrating the collapse of the old beliefs provides Milton with the opportunity to use them for his verses' own adornment. Compare to Poe's "Sonnet—To Science," where again the dryad is banished from the wood, but by a different force.

Finch, "The Spleen"

Wordsworth, "The World Is Too Much with Us": Compare the solace Wordsworth seeks in a "creed outworn" to other uses the poets on this list find for classical myths. Ask students to reflect on the difference between such capitalized powers as "Nature" and the "Sea" to "Proteus" and "Triton."

Keats, "On First Looking into Chapman's Homer" and "To Homer": Keats links blind Homer's vision with a special access to the Greek deities. Compare what Keats reads Homer for, as suggested in these sonnets, with what Tennyson and Pound read him for, as suggested in their poems based on Homeric epic in the next section.

Poe, "Sonnet—To Science": If Poe berates science for destroying mythology, why does he still use mythological figures such as "Old Time"? "Science" herself becomes a mythological figure with an appropriate ancestry: you might ask students who Science's other parent might be, on the model of Keats's Grecian Urn as foster-child of silence and slow time. What is the function of the hint of the myth of Prometheus in lines 3–4?

Poe, "To Helen": A woman who is like the women of classical myth is also like a work of art, a posed statue. In the stasis and balance of the last stanza in particular, the poem may be compared with Bogan's "Medusa" and Yeats's "Leda and the Swan."

Tennyson, "The Lotos-Eaters," "Ulysses" (*CD-ROM Link), and "Tithonus"

Roberts, "Marsyas"

Yeats, "Leda and the Swan"

Robinson, "Miniver Cheevy": What values did Miniver hold when he "dreamed of Thebes and Camelot, / And Priam's neighbors"?

Pound, Canto I ("And then went down to the ship")

Bogan, "Medusa": Does Medusa's gaze turn the world into timeless art or sterile, deathly stasis? Compare the unmoving scene in the poem

with the narrative liveliness of the painting in Auden's "Musée des Beaux Arts."
W. C. Williams, From "Asphodel, That Greeny Flower"
H. D., From "The Walls Do Not Fall"
Kavanagh, "Epic"
Auden, "Musée des Beaux Arts"
Merwin, "Odysseus"

B. *Other Mythologies*

Beowulf: An interesting case, as both pagan and Christian mythology mingle, the latter layered over the former.
Yeats, "The Stolen Child" and "The Circus Animals' Desertion"
Graves, "To Juan at the Winter Solstice" and "The White Goddess"
Wilbur, "Seed Leaves"
Hill, From *Mercian Hymns*
Glück, "Gretel in Darkness"
Erdrich, "I Was Sleeping Where the Black Oaks Move"

8.3 The Bible

How do poets treat classical tales differently from biblical tales? Why is the Book of Genesis such a fruitful source for poetry?

Anonymous, "Adam Lay I-bounden"
Skelton, "Phillip Sparow
Spenser, *The Faerie Queene*, Book 1
M. Sidney, "Psalm 58"
Lanyer, From *Salve Deus Rex Judaeorum*
The Massachusetts Bay Psalm Book, "Psalm 58"
Finch, "Adam Posed"
Smart, "Psalm 58"
Clough, "The Latest Decalogue"
Howe, "Battle-Hymn of the Republic"
Anonymous, "Ezekiel Saw the Wheel"
Dickinson, #59 ("A little East of Jordan") and #1545 ("The Bible is an antique Volume—")
Yeats, "The Second Coming"
Stevens, "Peter Quince at the Clavier"
Hope, "Imperial Adam"
Judith Wright, "Eve to Her Daughters"
Gascoyne, "Ecce Homo"
Donald Hall, From "The One Day," "Prophecy"

T. Hughes, "Theology"
Wilner, "Reading the Bible Backwards"
Glück, "The Garden"

8.4 Myth and History as Moral Compasses

Mythological allusion is not only decorative or illustrative. It can also be used to point out the failings of the present world, either in comparison with a mythic past or under the pretense of retelling a story from that past. In the following four poems, what are the contemporary problems and what are their mythological solutions/disguises?

Langland, *Piers Plowman*
Kavanagh, "Epic"
Gascoyne, "Ecce Homo"
Judith Wright, "Eve to Her Daughters"

CHAPTER 9

Influence and Intertextuality

9.1 Homage, Imitation, and Parody

It is not always easy to trace lines of influence from the collection of poems in an anthology, but it is vital that students understand that the tradition of poetry in English is one long running conversation—sometimes an argument, sometimes a genteel debate, sometimes a bravura comic contest. All of the following selections refer to other poems and poets, most of which are also represented in this anthology. Some we have grouped together, but most we have presented serially. Several of the poems are parodies not of other poems but of other kinds of texts, as is the case with **Porter's** "Consumer's Report." Clustering texts that show influence, imitation, and parody is a powerful way of bringing poetry to life for students and can open otherwise inaccessible poems to lively dialogue, both among themselves and among your students.

Skelton, "Phillip Sparow"
Whitney, "A Communication Which the Author Had to London, Before She Made Her Will"
P. Sidney, "What Length of Verse?"
Herrick, "Delight in Disorder" and Jonson, "Still To Be Neat": Herrick's poem is a parody of Jonson's, but students should see the admi-

ration in the parody. To bring this out, have your students also read Herrick's "An Ode for Him."

Gay, Songs from *The Beggar's Opera*, "Air X"
Leapor, "Mira's Will"
Tennyson, "The Lady of Shalott"
Clough, "The Latest Decalogue"
Lewis, "Song ('Come live with me and be my love')": Lewis parodies Marlowe's "The Passionate Shepherd to His Love" (*CD-ROM Link), but we also have Ralegh's contemporary parodic rejoinder, "The Nymph's Reply to the Shepherd." An exercise: after reading Marlowe's poem, have your class split into two groups, one to draft the woman's reply and the other to draft a contemporary "invitation" poem. After they read their drafts to each other, have them read Ralegh's and Lewis's poems. For this exercise to work, of course, it is important that students not be aware of the parodies before they try their own hands at them.
Roethke, "The Lost Son"
Justice, "Counting the Mad"
Koch, "Variations on a Theme by William Carlos Williams": Read this poem after reading its inspiration, W. C. Williams's "This Is Just to Say." *CD-ROM Link
Porter, "A Consumer's Report"
Mathews, "Histoire"
Harrison, "On Not Being Milton" and "A Kumquat for John Keats": Harrison does not exactly imitate or parody so much as invoke his major influences in order to shape his own rhetorical identity differently. How do Harrison's poems betray both admiration and anxiety?
Hass, "Tahoe in August"
Palmer, "Of this cloth doll which"

9.2 Translation and Revision

Can a poem translated from another language into English be an English poem in its own right? Even if you cannot teach the originals, you can use these poems to introduce different approaches to translation, perhaps also by bringing to the students' attention other translations of these poems for comparison. Questions of translation are useful for teaching lyric poetry in general: ask students which part of a poem they think would be the hardest to translate into another language, or which poets they think would be hardest to translate. Why might **Cummings** or **Dickinson** be harder to translate than **Stevens?** What different features of the poetry would likely be lost in translating a poem by **Wyatt** and a poem by **Blake?** What different features would be lost when an English poem is translated into French, Spanish, or German? Even students who have just a year or so of a foreign language might find it instructive to cast a stanza or two of an English poem into that language, or from that language into English (perhaps working collaboratively), and discuss the results. In conjunction with this topic, see **Keats's** "On First Looking into Chapman's Homer," about the experience of reading a formerly inaccessible poet through a good translation. Poems in the anthology that are translations—of varying degrees of accuracy and freedom—are listed here. Some may be more aptly called adaptations, variations, or imitations than translations. **Elizabeth Barrett Browning's** *Sonnets from the Portuguese* are not actually translations of Portuguese texts: why might a poet title her work as though they were English versions of works in another language?

Wyatt, "The Long Love, That in My Thought Doth Harbor": From the Italian of Petrarch. Compare Surrey's translation of the same sonnet.
Surrey, "Love, That Doth Reign and Live Within My Thought"
M. Sidney, "Psalm 58"; The Massachusetts Bay Psalm Book, "Psalm 58"; Smart, "Psalm 58"
Campion, "My Sweetest Lesbia"
Jonson, "Song: To Celia (I)": Lines 6–8 are recognizably versions of the same moment in Catullus that Campion draws upon in lines 3–7 of "My Sweetest Lesbia."
FitzGerald, "The Rubáiyát of Omar Khayyám of Naishápúr"
Yeats, "When You Are Old": From the French of Ronsard
Pound, "The Seafarer"
Wilbur, "Junk": Compare to Pound's version of Old English alliterative verse in "The Seafarer."
Merrill, From *The Book of Ephraim*
Kenney, "Aubade"

9.3 Poems that Reply to Other Poems

Occasionally poems reply to other poems directly, as in the exchange of **Marlowe's** "The Passionate Shepherd to His Love" (*CD-ROM Link) and **Ralegh's** "The Nymph's Reply to the Shepherd." Five more poems that reply to other poems are listed below. As an exercise, have your students track down the poems to which they reply.

Queen Elizabeth I, "[Ah silly pugg wert thou so sore afraid]"
Ralegh, "A Vision upon the Fairy Queen"
MacDiarmid, "Another Epitaph on an Army of Mercenaries"
Merrill, From *The Book of Ephraim*
Strand, From *Dark Harbor*, XVI

CHAPTER 10

Regional and Dialect Poetry

10.1 Regional Poetry

Regional poetry is tricky to define, and in some sense all poetry is regional just as all politics is local. Regional poetry is not exactly the same thing as landscape poetry (see section16.2 "Landscapes and Seascapes"), nor is it entirely coincident with ethnic or other group affiliation. One working definition might be: poetry rooted in place identity rather than group, class, or gender identity. Listed below are poems from the past two centuries that display a particularly strong sense of place. They may prove useful for a class in which you discuss the extent to which some poets identify with the land, or how different regions develop their own poetic traditions.

Wordsworth, "Lines Composed a Few Miles Above Tintern Abbey," *The Prelude*, (Book I), "She Dwelt Among the Untrodden Ways," "I Wandered Lonely As a Cloud," and "The Solitary Reaper": Wordsworth may be the father of regional poetry in English; he adopted the Welsh Lake District and the surrounding region and made the landscape itself integral to his poetic identity. To this day, students around the world are often introduced to Wordsworth and Coleridge under the sobriquet "The Lake District Poets."

Coleridge, "Frost at Midnight"

Emerson, "Concord Hymn," "Rhodora," "Ode (Inscribe to W. H. Channing)," and "The Snowstorm"; Longfellow, "The Jewish Cemetery at Newport" and "The Cross of Snow": The poetry of the New England Transcendentalists, while showing the influences of wide reading and cross-cultural fertilization (Emerson showed off what he had learned of Hinduism in poems such as "Brahma" and "Hamatreya," while Longfellow adapted the unique verse form of the Finnish epic *Kalevala* for his "Hiawatha"), is redolent of its regional roots. An exercise: have students compose brief verses (fixed or free, as they please) about a familiar battle-site, monument, or cemetery in the region where they grew up or have now adopted as adults.

Robinson, "Miniver Cheevy" and "Mr. Flood's Party"

Frost, "Mending Wall," "The Wood-Pile," "The Oven Bird," "Birches," "Stopping by Woods on a Snowy Evening," "The Gift Outright," and "Directive": How do Frost's poems make the New England farmlands, forests, and hills into a kind of collective character with whom the poet is engaged in continual conversation?

Jeffers, "Carmel Point"

Toomer, "Reapers" and "Harvest Song"; Brown, "Slim in Atlanta" and "Bitter Fruit of the Tree": How are race and region inextricably bound together by these poems of African-American culture in the rural south? Compare to L. Hughes's poetry of the northern, urban African-American scene during and immediately following the decades of the Great Migration in "The Weary Blues" (*CD-ROM Link), "Dream Variations," "Harlem," and "Theme for English B." What themes connect black life in north and south? How do the regions differently shape black experience?

R. S. Thomas, "Welsh Landscape" and "The View from the Window"; D. Thomas, "Fern Hill" *CD-ROM Link: How does the Welsh landscape figure differently in these poems than in the poetry of Wordsworth and Coleridge? Does a rooted ethnicity breed a stronger and/or more conflicted affiliation with a region than the affiliation of those outsiders who adopt an area as their own?

Hill, From *Mercian Hymns*

Snyder, "Above Pate Valley"; Hass, "Tahoe in August": How does the landscape of the mountainous western United States provide a common touchstone for these two very different poems?

Komunyakaa, "Banking Potatoes" and "Sunday Afternoons"

10.2 Dialect Poetry

All spoken language is spoken in one dialect or another: the Queen's English is a dialect as certainly as is the English of Queens, New York. Most poetry, however, even when written by members of ethnicities and/or classes with markedly marginalized dialects, tends to eschew the contractions, slang, phonetic spellings, and peculiarities of syntax unique to the poet's own native speech. The risks of writing deliberately in a marginal dialect are high: poetry identified as "dialect poetry" is often treated as a curiosity, a bit of odd exotica, of interest largely to anthropologists and other speakers of the dialect, but of little literary importance. This anthology, nonetheless, contains some fine examples of poetry in particular dialects. As an exercise, have your students try to draft a few lines in their "natural" speech and then translate those lines into formal, standardized English. What is gained and what is lost in the revision?

Burns, "To a Mouse," "Holy Willie's Prayer," "Green Grow the Rashes," "John Anderson, My Jo," and "A Red, Red Rose": Most of Burns's poems are written in the dialect known as Lowland Scots. You might point out to your students that Burns is considered the national poet of Scotland and is celebrated with his own holiday and a traditional meal, the Burns Supper. As a variation on the exercise just above, have students "normalize" Burns's verse and discuss what is lost in the process. Is the standardization of dialect a translation or a mutilation? And if it is a translation, was Frost correct in joking that "Poetry is what is lost in translation"?

Elliot, "The Flowers of the Forest"

Anonymous, "Go Down, Moses" and "Ezekiel Saw the Wheel"; P. L. Dunbar, "Little Brown Baby"; Brown, "Slim in Atlanta": James Weldon Johnson once argued against the use (and abuse) of dialect in African-American poetry, claiming that "Dialect has but two stops: humor and pathos." Do these poems display only humor and sentimentality? How is the recording of oral dialect in the anonymous spirituals different from Dunbar's educated-minstrel imitation of that dialect and Brown's satiric display of it?

Mew, "The Farmer's Bride"

CHAPTER 11

Poetry by Women

The concerns of women are at least as varied as the concerns of men, and the issues of class, ethnicity, and religion that divide or link the poetry of men also divide or link the poetry of women. Nevertheless, as real effort has been required to restore and maintain the visibility of women within the canon, the number and diversity of women poets in this anthology is of interest. The project of recovering lost voices continues, and more than half of the poets listed below are new to this edition of the shorter *Norton Anthology of Poetry*. We recommend devoting at least a class or two to tracing both the continuity and the diversity of themes in women's poetry in English throughout the past several centuries. This chapter should not, however, be taken as an encouragement to teach women's poetry as a segregated preserve, nor to assume that issues of gender overwhelm other issues in poems written by women.

The selection below names all the women included in the shorter edition of the anthology. We have paused at some to suggest possible approaches and connections for teaching their poems in the context of other poems—by women and by men—in the anthology. Otherwise, we have simply listed poets by their surnames, although their work may be more particularly referred to in comparisons elsewhere in the list. See also section 17, "Gender Relations."

Askew, "The Ballad Which Anne Askewe Made and Sang When She Was in Newgate": Askew's poem can be usefully placed in context either of other ballads, both popular and literary, or of other poems composed during imprisonment or forced confinement, such as "Tichborne's Elegy."

Queen Elizabeth I: Elizabeth is not the only aristocratic woman poet represented in this anthology—Mary Sidney, Lady Mary Wroth, Lady Mary Wortley Montagu, and Anne Finch, Countess of Winchilsea, are others—but she is the only monarch or head of state of either gender here. Do Elizabeth's poems seem more at home among those by aristocrats such as Surrey, the Sidneys, Ralegh, Rochester, etc., than they do sandwiched between works of "commoners," such as Askew's ballad (prior to her execution as a heretical witch) and Whitney's satirical "will" to London? How do power, gender, and genre intersect in Elizabeth's courtly, coterie verses "When I Was Fair and Young" (*CD-ROM Link), "[The doubt of future foes exiles my present joy]," and "[Ah silly pugg wert thou so sore afraid]" as compared to Askew's prison ballad and Whitney's London "will"?

Whitney

M. Sidney

Lanyer

Wroth, From "A Crowne of Sonnets Dedicated to Love": Compare the tropes employed by Wroth (e.g., Love as labyrinth, thread, and tutor) to those employed in any of the masculine love-sonnet cycles of Spenser, P. Sidney, Daniel, Drayton, and Shakespeare. It might also be useful to leap forward three centuries and compare the Wroth sonnets to E. B. Browning's *Sonnets from the Portugese* and Millay's sonnets "Euclid Alone Has Looked on Beauty Bare" and "I, Being Born a Woman and Distressed." Or compare the dark tones of Wroth's "Song ('Love a child is ever crying')" with Donne's bitter "Song ('Go and catch a falling star')." Finally, you might compare the terms of Jonson's tribute to Shakespeare, "To the Memory of My Beloved, the Author Mr. William Shakespeare," with those of his tribute to Wroth, "A Sonnet to the Noble Lady, the Lady Mary Wroth." How do conventions of class and gender differently shape his language of praise?

Bradstreet: You might want to begin a unit on women poets with selections on poetry or artistic creation, such as Bradstreet's "The Author to Her Book," Cavendish's "An Apology for Writing So Much upon This Book," Dickinson's #1129 ("Tell all the Truth but tell it slant—"), Moore's "Poetry" (*CD-ROM Link), and Rich's "Aunt Jennifer's Tigers."

Cavendish

Philips, "Epitaph": Compare to Jonson's epitaph "On My First Son." How does Jonson's figuring of his son as his best piece of work differ from Philips' manner of mourning for her son? Or compare "To My Excellent Lucasia, on Our Friendship" with other poems of male and female friendship in the collection. How does Philips toy with conventional gender expectations in her praise of "Lucasia"?

Behn, "The Disappointment": Can be taught as a sequel/rejoinder to Donne's "The Flea" or Marvell's "To His Coy Mistress": the poetics of seventeenth-century sexuality was not entirely circumscribed by clever male conquests of coy female chastity.

Finch

Montagu, "The Lover: A Ballad": Could be taught in the context of other poems in which women define what they do and do not want from men, including Millay's "I, Being Born a Woman and Distressed," Parker's "One Perfect Rose," Rich's "Living in Sin."

Leapor, "Mira's Will": Compare to Whitney's "The Manner of her Will, & What She Left to London, and to All Those in It, at Her Departing."

Elliot

Barbauld, "The Rights of Woman" *CD-ROM Link

C. Smith

Wheatley, "On Being Brought from Africa to America": How does Wheatley attempt to reconstruct a shattered identity within the culture that both enslaved her and nurtured her art? The costs of the struggle to salvage a whole identity from the crucible of violence and dislocation are also displayed in other poems by African-American women in this anthology, including Brooks's "kitchenette building," Lorde's "Coal," Wilner's "Reading the Bible Backwards," and Dove's "Parsley" (*CD-ROM Link). Wheatley's poem can also be read with L. Hughes's "The Negro Speaks of Rivers" and Cullen's "Heritage": what are the peculiar problems of identity that continue to resonate from the cultural ruptures of the forced African diaspora and how does each of these three poems attempt a different resolution?

Tighe

Hemans

E. B. Browning

Brontë: You might ask the class to speculate about why "No Coward Soul Is Mine" was one of Dickinson's favorite poems.

Howe

Dickinson

C. Rossetti: Compare "Song ('When I am dead, my dearest')" to Dickinson's poems spoken from the grave ("I heard a Fly buzz—when I died—" and "Because I could not stop for Death—") and to Plath's "Lady Lazarus."

Mew, "The Farmer's Bride": Compare to Lawrence's "Love on the Farm." Both poems mingle suggestions of the casual, earthy brutality of farm life with human sexual tension. How and how much do their perspectives differ?

A. Lowell

Stein, From *Stanzas in Meditation:* Stein's work is among the most unconventional and formally innovative in the collection. A class discussion could easily be devoted to formal experiment in poetry by women, including such gender/genre transgressions as Askew's trimeter prison ballad, Whitney's and Leapor's "wills," Bradstreet's and Cavendish's prologues to their books, Wroth's "crowne" of love sonnets, Dickinson's mutations of common meter, H. D.'s spartan free verse, Moore's syllabics, Bishop's experiments with sestina and villanelle, and Brooks's razored monosyllables in "We Real Cool" (*CD-ROM Link).

H. D., "Helen": How does H. D.'s figuring of the tragedy of Helen's beauty differ from the stock figure of "the face that launched a thousand ships" in male-authored poems, from Landor's "Past Ruined Ilion Helen Lives" to Yeats's "Among School Children" and "No Second Troy"?

Moore

Millay

Parker

Bogan, "Man Alone": How does this poem play on its simultaneous tropes, of the book as the reader's mirror and the woman as mirror for the specular vision of her male lover, in order to destabilize both conventions?

S. Smith, "Mr. Over," "Not Waving but Drowning," and "Pretty": Compare Smith's darkly ironic humor with Parker's in "Résumé" and "One Perfect Rose." In what ways can these poems be considered anything but "light verse"?

Jacobsen, "Hourglass": How does this celebration of life, written near the end of an exceptionally long life, wrest new and surprising meaning from the *carpe diem* convention so beloved of male-authored seduction poems such as Herrick's "To the Virgins, to Make Much of Time" and Marvell's "To His Coy Mistress"?

Bishop

Rukeyser, "Ballad of Orange and Grape": Is there any level at which this poem is also a ballad of male and female? How does the whole poem ironize conventions of binary opposition through its central motif of confused distinctions?

Swenson

Judith Wright, "Woman to Man" and "Eve to Her Daughters": Compare both poems to each other, as well as to Barbauld's "The Rights of Woman" (*CD-ROM Link) and Wilner's "Reading the Bible Backwards." For an interesting long-range historical comparison, place

"Eve to Her Daughters" in the context of the anonymous fifteenth-century lyric "Adam Lay I-bounden." How does the Promethean theme of Adam's desire to play with fire lead to the theological concept of *felix culpa* in one instance and to nuclear armageddon in the other?

Page

Brooks: Compare the picture of domestic poverty in "kitchenette building" with the apparently cozy but profoundly sorrowful rustic kitchen of Bishop's "Sestina." Or, compare Brooks's poem on childbirth, "the birth in a narrow room," with Plath's "Morning Song" or Bradstreet's "Before the Birth of One of Her Children."

Clampitt

Guest

Van Duyn, "Letters from a Father": Compare with Clampitt's poem about her father, "Beethoven, Opus 111," and Plath's caustic "Daddy."

Levertov, "Caedmon": How does Levertov connect to and play upon the Old English poem that opens this anthology, Cædmon's "Hymn"?

Jennings

Sexton

Rich, "Diving into the Wreck" *CD-ROM Link: How does Rich use pronouns to blur and corrode deep gender distinctions? Compare this poem to both the earlier portraits of women snared, "Aunt Jennifer's Tigers" and "Living in Sin," and the later excerpt 8 ("A woman wired in memories") from "Eastern War Time": ask your students to trace the figures of entanglement and entrapment through all these poems and then to look for language that suggests hope of release.

MacPherson

Plath, "Morning Song": How does this poem ironize the conventional cliches of motherhood?

Adcock

Lorde

Wilner

Atwood

Glück, "Gretel in Darkness" and "The Garden": How does Glück uncover and recover the undersides of myth and fairytale in these two poems? Compare to H. D.'s "Helen" and Judith Wright's "Eve to Her Daughters."

Boland

Graham

Dove

Schnackenberg

Duffy, "Warming Her Pearls": Duffy's poem foregrounds ethnic and class distinctions, but it does so within the context of two women's relationship—oppressively professional but peculiarly intimate—constructed by those distinctions. How are the roles of feminity formed by class in this poem? How are the differing class roles bound together by gender?

Erdrich, "Birth": Compare to Plath's "Morning Song" and Bradstreet's "Before the Birth of One of Her Children."

Zarin

CHAPTER 12

Poetry by Marginalized Groups

As with the preceding section listing the women poets in the anthology's shorter edition, this chapter is intended to highlight counter-traditions that might otherwise be overlooked, not to winnow out marginalized poets and then reinscribe their marginal status by placing them in a quarantined preserve, apart from the "regular" poets of dominant classes and culture. Most of the poets and poems listed in the sections immediately below appear elsewhere in this guide as well, whether they illustrate points of versification, development, and rhetoric or exemplify particular issues and topics. We hope that by gathering them together here, however, we can encourage discussions with and among students that highlight the distinctive issues and contributions of these groups and of their infragroup traditions. For additional cross-references, see also the sections on "Influence and Intertextuality" (9.1–3), "Social and Political Protest" (18.2), "Rich and Poor" (18.3), and "Race and Ethnicity" (19.1–3).

12.1 "Peasant" and "Blue-Collar" Poets

This is a nebulous category, one not easily filled by a quick check of the historical race, gender, or nationality of each poet. However, class and economic status are crucial factors in the lives of many poets and in the content, rhetoric, and reception of their poems. Here, then, is a small selection of poets and poems that lend themselves to classroom discussion of class issues:

Burns: Listed also in section 10, "Regional and Dialect Poetry," and section 12.2, "Celtic Poets Writing in English"; you may want to emphasize for your students the fact that Burns was, during his lifetime, a celebrity for a while as a "farmer poet." Like the African-American poets Wheatley and Dunbar, British poets of the "lower orders" such as Burns and Clare (below) were often feted as freakish wonders and then ignored, especially if they did not continue to write verse that seemed appropriately docile and imitative of the canonical works of the dominant culture. Although Burns is best known for his love lyrics in Scots dialect, three poems from this collection that would be relevant here are "To a Mouse," "Holy Willie's Prayer," and perhaps "John Anderson, My Jo."

Clare: Also celebrated by the educated classes as a marvel, Clare was called the "Peasant Poet." The three selections in the shorter edition do not elucidate Clare's class concerns well—he wrote extensively in protest of the "Enclosure Laws" that spelled doom for the medieval tradition of "common" grazing lands. All three poems, however, may be compared with the poems of Burns above; "Badger," in particular, gives us a glimpse of a peasant farmer's perspective on nature. You might point out that in a Wordsworth poem set in a rural landscape, Clare or Burns themselves might be appropriated as archetypal figures like Lucy or "The Solitary Reaper," half human, half objects rooted in the soil, "rolled round with rocks and earth and trees."

Whitman: Few poets have made such a cause for celebration of their working-class status as Whitman does. Sections 1 (*CD-ROM Link) and 24 of "Song of Myself" are especially apt here, as is "Crossing Brooklyn Ferry." An exercise that works well with classes of working and/or commuting students: have students, in small groups, compose a few lines of their own that detail the people they might see commuting to school or work, on a bus, subway, or even highway, and then read and discuss their own lines in comparison with each other's and Whitman's.

Hayden, "Those Winter Sundays"
James Wright, "A Note Left in Jimmy Leonard's Shack"
Harrison, "A Kumquat for John Keats"
Heaney, "Digging"
Komunyakaa, "Banking Potatoes"
Muldoon, "Gathering Mushrooms"

12.2 Celtic Poets Writing in English

It is important to remind students that the Celtic languages have accumulated centuries of recorded poetry of their own, and that Celtic poetry in English (or, put differently, English-language poetry by ethnic Celts who may or may not have learned English as their first or only tongue) by no means comprises the whole of the Celtic poetic tradition. Nonetheless, the contributions of Celtic poets to the English-language canon are remarkable. The following list pauses occasionally to single out poems in which Celtic themes, culture, or intertextual references are prominent. (Again, see also the topical units in section 19, "Race and Ethnicity.")

Burns, "Green Grow the Rashes"
Yeats, "The Stolen Child," "The Wild Swans at Coole," "Easter 1916" (*CD-ROM Link), "Among School Children," "Crazy Jane Talks with the Bishop," "Under Ben Bulben"
MacDiarmid, From "In Memoriam James Joyce"
Lewis
Kavanagh, From "The Great Hunger"
MacNeice, "Bagpipe Music"
R. S. Thomas, "Welsh Landscape"
D. Thomas, "Fern Hill" *CD-ROM Link
Ormond
Heaney, "Digging," "Punishment," From "Station Island"
Mahon, "A Disused Shed in Co. Wexford"
Boland, "That the Science of Cartography Is Limited" *CD-ROM Link
Muldoon, "Gathering Mushrooms"
Duffy, "Warming Her Pearls"

12.3 African-American Poets

The first two poets named on this list, **Wheatley** and **Dunbar,** were both celebrated and marginalized by educated white society, which praised their gifts for versification in the way that Samuel Johnson was reported to have compared a woman's preaching to a dog walking on two legs—not so much that it was done well, as a marvel it was done at all. In keeping with this attitude, white audiences preferred those **Wheatley** and **Dunbar** poems that reinforced their own opinions. This history later led some black poets and critics to deny that **Wheatley's** heroic couplets stuffed with allusions to Graeco-Roman mythology and **Dunbar's** sentimental or humorous quatrains in minstrel dialect belonged to any true tradition of African-American poetry. Ask your students, both before and after reading some of the poems below, what they know of African-American poetry and what they might consider its traditional themes. Discuss how reading these poems reshapes their expectations. (Again, for further discussion and exercises, turn to the topical units in section 19, "Race and Ethnicity.") Other useful subjects for discussion: How do issues of gender intersect with issues of race in African-American poetry? Do class and economic status figure prominently in any of these poems? How do themes of national (particularly American) identity surface and resurface?

Wheatley, "On Being Brought from Africa to America" and "To S. M., a Young African Painter, On Seeing His Works"
Anonymous, Spirituals, "Go Down, Moses" and "Ezekiel Saw the Wheel"
Dunbar, "Little Brown Baby" and "Sympathy"
Toomer, "Reapers" and "Harvest Song"
Brown, "Slim in Atlanta" and "Bitter Fruit of the Tree"
L. Hughes: All of Hughes's selections are valuable, but "The Negro Speaks of Rivers," "Song for a Dark Girl," and "Theme for English B" may prove especially so. Discussions of "The Weary Blues" and Hughes's life and work are on *The Norton Poetry Workshop CD-ROM.*
Cullen, "Heritage" and "Incident"
Hayden, "Night, Death, Mississippi"
Brooks: All selections, but especially "kitchenette building," "the rites for Cousin Vit" and "We Real Cool" *CD-ROM Link
Baraka, "An Agony. As Now."
Lorde, "Coal"
Wilner, "Reading the Bible Backwards"
Komunyakaa, "Banking Potatoes" and "Sunday Afternoons"
Dove, "Parsley" *CD-ROM Link

12.4 Other American Poets of Ethnic Minorities Who Write in English

NATIVE AMERICAN

Momaday, "Headwaters," "The Eagle-Feather Fan," "The Gift," and "Two Fighters"
Erdrich, "I Was Sleeping Where the Black Oaks Move" and "Birth"

LATIN-AMERICAN

Soto, "Not Knowing"

ASIAN-AMERICAN

Lee, "Persimmons" *CD-ROM Link

CHAPTER 13

Postcolonial and Commonwealth Poetry

The categories of Postcolonial and Commonwealth poetry are novel to most students in the United States. Many students will not be aware of the national backgrounds of most or any of the poets below, except where cued by topics in the poems, and perhaps not even then. Most of the names are not yet familiar to readers in the United States, although a few, such as **Soyinka, Lowry, Atwood, Ondaatje,** and **Walcott,** are well known to poetry lovers in this country. As a simple eye-opener, it may be worth your while simply to give students a global tour of these poets who hail from neither the U.S. nor the British Isles, but who have written vibrant, important work in our common language. In the lists below, we have highlighted poems that particularly relate to national or (Post)colonial issues.

13.1 African Poets

Campbell
Soyinka, "Telephone Conversation"

13.2 Australian and New Zealander Poets

Hope, "Australia" and "Inscription for a War"
Judith Wright
Baxter, "New Zealand"

Porter, "A Consumer's Report"
Adcock
Murray, "Noonday Axeman"

13.3 Canadian Poets

Roberts, "Marsyas"
Pratt
Birney, "Bushed"
Lowry
Layton, "Berry Picking"
Page
MacPherson, "The Swan"
Atwood, "At the Tourist Center in Boston"
Ondaatje

13.4 Caribbean Poets

Brathwaite, "Ancestors," 1–3
Walcott, "A Far Cry from Africa" (*CD-ROM Link), From "The Schooner *Flight*," and From *Omeros*, "Chapter XXX"

III. Topics

CHAPTER 14

Poetry and Poets

14.1 Poetry

Every poem, of course, espouses its own implicit ars poetica; these poems explicitly take up the topic of the poetic imagination. (See also section 14.2, "The Muse.")

Shakespeare, Sonnet 55 ("Not marble, nor the gilded monuments"): Do twentieth-century poets continue to uphold this sonnet's claim for the immortalizing powers of poetry?
Jonson, "A Fit of Rhyme Against Rhyme"
Herbert, "Jordan (I)"
Bradstreet, "The Prologue"
Cavendish, "An Apology for Writing So Much upon This Book"
Collins, "Ode on the Poetical Character"
Leapor, "The Epistle of Deborah Dough"
Wordsworth, "Nuns Fret Not at Their Convent's Narrow Room"
Housman, " 'Terence, This Is Stupid Stuff . . .' "
Yeats, "The Circus Animals' Desertion"
W. C. Williams, "Asphodel, That Greeny Flower"
Moore, "Poetry" *CD-ROM Link: What is the "raw material of poetry," according to this poem? In what sense might the short quotations Moore weaves into the poem be considered "raw material"? What might Ammons or Silko consider poetry's "raw material"?

Lewis, "Where are the War Poets?"
O'Hara, "Why I Am Not a Painter"
T. Hughes, "The Thought-Fox"
Strand, "The Prediction"
Heaney, "Digging"
Palmer, "Fifth Prose"

14.2 The Muse

If we define a muse as any female figure whom the poet invokes or to whom he pleads for inspiration and guidance, we will find that the myth of the muse persists from the earliest poetry to the present day. Must a muse be female? Can women poets have muses? In "The Author to Her Book," **Anne Bradstreet** calls her poetry her "offspring"; do male poets also think of their poems as children they have borne? Compare **Jonson's** "On My First Son," in which he calls his son "his best piece of poetry." This topic is related to questions of occasion; that is, to the larger issues of what occasions a poem, brings it into existence, or motivates the poet to write it (see section 7.1.A, "Occasional Poetry").

Gascoigne, "Gascoigne's Lullaby": What womanly power of voice does Gascoigne wish to claim for himself? Compare Bradstreet's comparison of her book with a child in "The Author to Her Book," and Sidney's description of himself as "great with child to speak" in the poem below.
P. Sidney, Astrophel and Stella, 1 ("Loving in truth, and fain in verse my love to show"): Has Sidney followed his muse's advice in the writing of this poem?
Lanyer, From *Salve Deus Rex Judaeorum*
Milton, from *Paradise Lost*, Book 1 [The Invocation]
Bradstreet, "The Author to Her Book"
Wordsworth, "The Solitary Reaper"
Whitman, "Out of the Cradle Endlessly Rocking"
Stevens, "The Idea of Order at Key West"
Nemerov, "Boy with Book of Knowledge"
Merwin, "The Drunk in the Furnace": In what sense might the drunk be considered a muse figure? How is he like the singing reaper in Wordsworth's poem?
Hecht, "The Ghost in the Martini"

14.3 Tributes to Poets

In these poems tribute is paid by one poet to an earlier poet, in some cases one who could not have been a friend or contemporary. How is the eulogist's task different from the elegist's—that is, when what is at stake is not, as in an elegy, finding consolation for a personal loss, but declaring a poetic heritage?

Surrey, "Wyatt Resteth Here"
Ralegh, "A Vision upon the Fairy Queen"
Jonson, "To the Memory of My Beloved, the Author Mr. William Shakespeare" and "A Sonnet to the Noble Lady, the Lady Mary Wroth"
Carew, "An Elegy upon the Death of the Dean of Paul's, Dr. John Donne"
Collins, "Ode on the Poetical Character": Why does this ode, which begins with a worshipful nod to Spenser, end up as a tribute to Milton? How does Collins use Spenser to help praise Milton?
C. Smith, "To the shade of Burns"
Keats, "On Sitting Down to Read *King Lear* Once Again" and "To Homer"
Arnold, "Shakespeare": Compare the kinds of wisdom Arnold and Keats attribute to Shakespeare. Unlike Jonson's and Milton's tributes to Shakespeare, these nineteenth-century poems do not treat Shakespeare chiefly as a dramatist—there's a lesson here about how views of a poet's canon and achievements may change over time.
Dickinson #569 ("I reckon—when I count at all—")
MacDiarmid, From "In Memoriam James Joyce"
Auden, "In Memory of W. B. Yeats" *CD-ROM Link
Berryman, From "Homage to Mistress Bradstreet"
Strand, From *Dark Harbor*, XVI
Harrison, "On Not Being Milton" and "A Kumquat for John Keats": Harrison's poems are less tributes than efforts to mark difference. (See also section 9, "Influence and Intertextuality.") Heaney, From "Station Island": Compare with MacDiarmid's "In Memoriam James Joyce."

CHAPTER 15

Daily Life

Your students are likely to believe that humdrum, quotidian existence is anything but the stuff of poetry. So it can be rewarding to show them just how many successful poems have been written that celebrate, bemoan, or explore daily routine. For starters, have them read Berryman's Dream Song 14 ("Life, friends, is boring. We must not say so"), and ask them why the adjective "heavy" in his phrase "I am heavy bored" is more effective than the more usual adverbs "terribly" or "awfully" would be. What tone of address does the opening line establish and how? Why does the feel of a wry, intimate confidence suit the poem perfectly? Have the students ever thought of such address as being suitable for poetry? Perhaps compare with Dickinson's dolorous poem #258 ("There's a certain Slant of light"): see if your students notice that she also uses a trope of oppressive weight, "heft."

15.1 Work

In teaching an introductory class in poetry it is sometimes hard to avoid leaving students with the impression that poetry is concerned entirely with matters of leisure hours—love, art, mourning, meditative walks, and moments of contemplation—and not with the daily, tiring, unremarkable time spent working for a living. Such an impression tends to suggest that poetry, too, is a luxury, the result of idle hours, to be read in idle hours or in English classes. Insofar as some of the poems listed below suggest that the various kinds of work they describe may also be figures for the poet's labors, they may help to open discussion about what kinds of work the reading and writing of poetry is, as well as what kinds of work it may treat. (See also sections 12.1, on " 'Peasant' and 'Blue-Collar' Poets," and 16.8, "Farm Life.")

Frost, "Mending Wall" and "The Wood-Pile"
Williams, "The Red Wheelbarrow"
Toomer, "Reapers"
Ammons, "Silver"
Murray, "Noonday Axeman"
Heaney, "Digging"
Kenney, "Apples on Champlain"
Muldoon, "Gathering Mushrooms"

15.2 Home and Family

Jonson, "Inviting a Friend to Supper"
Bradstreet, "Here Follows Some Verses upon the Burning of Our House July 10th, 1666": What aspects of domestic comfort does Bradstreet have to dismiss before she can fully feel that the destruction of her house responds to her "desire" (line 6) and is a blessing?
Coleridge, "Frost at Midnight"
R. Browning, "Home-Thoughts, From Abroad"
Meredith, From *Modern Love*, 17 ("At dinner, she is hostess, I am host")
Mew, "The Farmer's Bride"
Frost, "The Hill Wife"
Williams, "Danse Russe" and "This Is Just to Say" (*CD-ROM Link): Compare the former to Coleridge's "Frost at Midnight," where again a father is awake in the house while his family sleeps.
Roethke, "My Papa's Waltz": Students often find this poem disturbing. Does it represent a fond memory of a gruff but loving father or a painful recollection of an abusive drunkard? Is the domestic scene pictured here boisterously cozy or on the edge of violence? Encourage your students to voice their choices, but then challenge them to point to the specific words, phrases, and rhythms that support their views.
Bishop, "Sestina"
Hayden, "Those Winter Sundays"
Brooks, "kitchenette building," "the birth in a narrow room," and "the rites for Cousin Vit"
Larkin, "Talking in Bed": Compare with Bishop's warm invocation of archetypal parents' voices in "The Moose."

Merrill, "The Broken Home"
Jennings, "My Grandmother"

15.3 Children and Childhood

Also see section 4.3.B, "Elegy," for poems on the deaths of children.

Blake, From *Songs of Innocence*, "Introduction," "The Lamb," and "The Little Black Boy": How does Blake use the black child's voice to suggest both his aspirations and the oppressive society that has shaped his vision of heaven?
Wordsworth, "It Is a Beauteous Evening," "My Heart Leaps Up," and "Ode: Intimations of Immortality"
Coleridge, "Frost at Midnight": Compare to Lowell's "Harriet," in which another father watches by the bed of his sleeping child.
Whitman, "Out of the Cradle Endlessly Rocking": Compare to Wordsworth's "Ode: Intimations of Immortality," another account of a childhood encounter with nature that shaped the adult poet.
Dickinson #613 ("The shut me up in Prose—")
Yeats, "The Stolen Child"
P. L. Dunbar, "Little Brown Baby": Compare to Blake's "The Little Black Boy." Why does the father deliberately scare his baby with talk of the "buggahman"?
Frost, "Birches"
Lawrence, "Piano"
Roethke, "My Papa's Waltz": See section 15.2, "Home and Family."
Bishop, "Sestina"
Hayden, "Those Winter Sundays": Compare the picture of love between a father and son in Roethke's "My Papa's Waltz."
D. Thomas, "Fern Hill" *CD-ROM Link
R. Lowell, "Harriet"
Nemerov, "Boy with Book of Knowledge"
Merrill, "The Broken Home"
Kinnell, "After Making Love We Hear Footsteps"
Komunyakaa, "Sunday Afternoons"
Zarin, "The Ant Hill"

15.4 Youth and Age

Gascoigne, "Gascoigne's Lullaby,"
"Tichborne, "Tichborne's Elegy": Compare to Keats's "When I Have Fears" and "This Living Hand." Woody Allen once joked that getting older wasn't so bad "when you consider the alternative": how do these poems by young men facing death illustrate the hard truth behind

the joke? Compare them also with poems written by men lamenting their ages, such as "Gascoigne's Lullaby" and Justice's "Men at Forty."
Shakespeare, Sonnet 3 ("Look in thy glass and tell the face thou viewest"): Compare with Hardy's poem below. Also, Sonnet 73 ("That time of year thou mayst in me behold")
Burns, "John Anderson, My Jo"
Hardy, "I Look into My Glass"
Housman, "To an Athlete Dying Young"
Yeats, "When You Are Old," "The Wild Swans at Coole," and "Among School Children": All three of these poems, written at various stages in the poet's life, involve images of Maud Gonne, the fiery Irish patriot whom Yeats pursued (unsuccessfully) for years. Compare the imagining of her as she will be in her old age in "When You Are Old" with the imagining of her as she is and was in her youth in "Among School Children."
Frost, "Provide, Provide": Compare Housman, "To an Athlete Dying Young."
Moore, "What Are Years?"
Eliot, "The Love Song of J. Alfred Prufrock": Point out to your students that this poem of middle-aged angst was composed by Eliot between the ages of nineteen and twenty-one. Can poetry of aging be successfully written by the young? This can be a lively discussion question in a class with mixed older and younger students.
Jacobsen, "Hourglass"
D. Thomas, "Do Not Go Gentle into That Good Night"
Van Duyn, "Letters from a Father"
Larkin, "Sad Steps"
Hecht, "The Ghost in the Martini"
Justice, "Men at Forty"
Hill "The Guardians"

A. *Birthdays*

Most students will have received or sent birthday greetings, and you might ask them to bring in some greeting-card verse to compare its methods and conventions with those of the poems below. Most of the poems on this list mark in gloomy terms the poet's arrival at a midpoint or crisis in life. How is writing a poem for your own birthday different from writing one on someone else's?

Milton, "On the Morning of Christ's Nativity," "How Soon Hath Time," and "When I Consider How My Life is Spent"
Swift, "Stella's Birthday"
Byron, "On This Day I Complete My Thirty-sixth Year"

Housman, "Loveliest of Trees, the Cherry Now"
Pound, "The River-Merchant's Wife: a Letter": Although this is not exactly a birthday poem, the speaker's recounting of each transition in each year—"At fourteen I married My Lord you. . . . At fifteen I stopped scowling. . . . At sixteen you departed"—amounts to the kind of reminiscence often occasioned by birthdays.
Justice, "Men at Forty"
Snodgrass, From *Heart's Needle*, 2 ("Late April and you are three; today")

15.5 Times of Day

A. Morning

To what kinds of reflections and anxieties are morning poems prone? How do they differ from the regrets and fears common to many of the night poems listed in section 15.6.B ?

Donne, "The Sun Rising"
Herrick, "Corinna's Going A-Maying"
Wordsworth, "Composed upon Westminster Bridge, September 3, 1802"
Tennyson, "In Memoriam A. H. H.," section 11 ("Calm is the morn without a sound")
Stevens, "Sunday Morning" *CD-ROM Link
Williams, "Danse Russe"
Rosenberg, "Break of Day in the Trenches": How does this poem ironize our conventional associations that link the dawn with renewal and hope?
Warren, "Masts at Dawn"
Plath, "Morning Song"
Kenney, "Aubade": Compare to Donne's "The Sun Rising," which is also an aubade, or morning song of a lover who laments the arrival of the dawn that means the end of a night of love.

B. Night

What special energies does night release, or what special knowledge does it give access to? Night may be a time of unusual serenity that yields inner peace or a sense of community (**Wroth, Finch, Wordsworth, Toomer**); or it may be a time of passion (**Dickinson**) or terror (**Hayden**); or it may create an otherworldly state of melancholy, suspension, and uncertainty (**Coleridge, Tennyson, Whitman, Frost, Schnackenberg**) that is often linked to thoughts of loss or death.

Anonymous, "Now Go'th Sun Under Wood"
Spenser, "Epithalamion": The bridegroom's wish for night (lines 278ff.) could be taught with this group. In which poems on this list is night associated with love?
P. Sidney, *Astrophil and Stella*, 31 ("With how sad steps, Oh Moon, thou climb'st the skies"): Compare with Daniel's love sonnet 49 ("Care-charmer Sleep, son of the sable Night").
Campion, "Now Winter Nights Enlarge"
Wroth, *Pamphilia to Amphilanthus*, 37 ("Night, welcome art thou to my mind destrest"): Compare to P. Sidney's and Daniel's nighttime love sonnets, listed just above.
Finch "A Nocturnal Reverie"
Blake, "To the Evening Star"
Wordsworth, "It Is a Beauteous Evening"
Coleridge, "Frost at Midnight"
Byron, "She Walks in Beauty"
Tennyson, "In Memoriam A. H. H.", sections 67 ("When on my bed the moonlight falls"), 95 ("By night we lingered on the lawn"), and 121 ("Sad Hesper o'er the buried sun"): Why is the relationship between night thoughts and sad or nostalgic memory so strong?
Whitman, "Vigil Strange I Kept on the Field One Night"
Dickinson, #249 ("Wild Nights—Wild Nights!")
Housman, "Crossing Alone the Nighted Ferry"
Frost, "Stopping by Woods on a Snowy Evening" and "Acquainted with the Night"
Bogan, "Night"
Auden, "As I Walked Out One Evening": Compare to Wordsworth's "It Is a Beauteous Evening" and Frost's "Acquainted with the Night"
Hayden, "Night, Death, Mississippi"
Schnackenberg, "Darwin in 1881"

15.6 Happiness and Dejection

This section includes a range of varied poems dealing with states of brief, ecstatic epiphanies, or of emotional crisis or psychic extremity. Most of the poems about dejection or joy will be love poems, elegies, or religious or devotional poems. How do these poems suggest that there are fashions or changing historical trends in joy and happiness? Is what the Romantics call "dejection" the same emotion we call "depression," or what Dickinson calls "a formal feeling" (poem #341)? Do tears, like maidenly blushes or fits of swooning, go in and out of fashion as expressions of feeling? As presented in these poems, which seems more an expression of historical conventions of feeling: happiness or dejection?

POEMS OF HAPPINESS

Anonymous, "The Cuckoo Song"
Milton, "L'Allegro"
Blake, From *Songs of Innocence*, "Introduction" ("Piping down the valleys wild")
Wordsworth, "I Wandered Lonely As a Cloud" and "Surprised by Joy"
Lear, "How Pleasant to Know Mr. Lear"
Williams, "Danse Russe"
Moore, "The Steeple-Jack"
Bishop, "The Moose"
Jarrell, "A Man Meets a Woman in the Street"
Kinnell, "After Making Love We Hear Footsteps"

POEMS OF DEJECTION

Anonymous, "Western Wind"
Wyatt, "My Galley"
Queen Elizabeth I, "[The doubt of future foes exiles my present joy]"
Donne, "A Valediction of Weeping"
Herbert, "Affliction (I)" and "The Flower"
Milton, "Il Penseroso"
Finch, "The Spleen"
Montagu, "A Receipt to Cure the Vapors"
Coleridge, "Dejection: An Ode"
Shelley, "Stanzas Written in Dejection, Near Naples"
Keats, "Ode on Melancholy"
Dickinson, #280 ("I felt a Funeral, in my Brain") and #341 ("After great pain, a formal feeling comes—")
Hardy, "The Darkling Thrush" and "During Wind and Rain"
Hopkins, "[No Worst, There Is None. Pitched Past Pitch of Grief]"
L. Hughes, "The Weary Blues" *CD-ROM Link
Bishop, "One Art"
Berryman, Dream Songs 29 ("There sat down, once, a thing on Henry's heart")
Larkin, "Sad Steps"

15.7 Technology and Modern Life

Whitman, "To a Locomotive in Winter"
Toomer, "Reapers"
Crane, "Proem: To Brooklyn Bridge"

Merrill, “The Victor Dog”
O’Hara, “The Day Lady Died”
Ashbery, “Melodic Trains”
Gunn, “On the Move”
Baraka, “In Memory of Radio”
Soyinka, “Telephone Conversation”
Murray, “Noonday Axeman” and “Morse”

15.8 Illness

Montagu, “A Receipt to Cure the Vapors”
Justice, “Counting the Mad”
Gunn, “The Missing”
Sissman, From “Dying: An Introduction”
Schnackenberg, “Darwin in 1881”

15.9 Food and Drink

Lyly, “Oh, For a Bowl of Fat Canary”
Jonson, “Inviting a Friend to Supper”
Tennyson, “The Lotos-Eaters”
Robinson, “Mr. Flood’s Party”
Stevens, “The Emperor of Ice-Cream”
W. C. Williams, “This Is Just to Say” *CD-ROM Link
Nash, “Reflections on Ice-breaking”
Layton, “Berry Picking”
Rukeyser, “Ballad of Orange and Grape”
Hecht, “The Ghost in the Martini”
Levertov, “O Taste and See”
Harrison, “A Kumquat for John Keats”
Komunyakaa, “Banking Potatoes”
Kenney, “Apples on Champlain”
Muldoon, “Gathering Mushrooms”
Daniel Hall, “Mangosteens”
Lee, “Persimmons” *CD-ROM Link

CHAPTER 16

Nature

16.1 Nature in General

Marvell, "The Garden": The garden into which the poet retreats from human toil and ambition might seem to be rather laboriously and skillfully designed and cultivated: is this a contradiction that needs to be resolved? Compare Swinburne's "A Forsaken Garden."

Wordsworth, "I Wandered Lonely As a Cloud": In which of the other poems on this list does nature seem to be chiefly something remembered or envisioned in the "inward eye"?

Whitman, "Song of Myself," section 6 ("A child said *What is the grass?* fetching it to me with full hands")

Hopkins, "God's Grandeur" and "Pied Beauty"

Frost "Design," "Come In," and "The Most of It"

Jeffers, "Carmel Point" : Might be studied along with Burns's "To a Mouse," where, again, to cultivate the land is to risk despoiling it in some way.

Auden, "In Praise of Limestone"

D. Thomas, "The Force That Through the Green Fuse Drives the Flower"

Wilbur, "Advice to a Prophet"

Schnackenberg, "Darwin in 1881"

16.2 Landscapes and Seascapes

The poems on this list figure sea and seashore in a variety of ways: the sea as a dynamic realm of constant destruction (**Cowper, Hardy, Williams**); as a force for preservation and transformation (**Shakespeare**); or as a mysterious, murky realm that counters, underlies, or mirrors our own solid earthly existence (**Eliot, Rich**). How do figurations of the sea and shore change over history? The present-day sense that the seashore is a natural place for meditative walks and romantic meetings (the popularity of this topos is evident from its commercial version in soft-focus photos on greeting cards of couples wandering on beaches in a sunset glow) seems not to emerge strongly in poetry until the nineteenth century (**Whitman, Arnold, Stevens**).

Anonymous, "The Seafarer"
Spenser, *Amoretti*, Sonnet 75 ("One day I wrote her name upon the strand") *CD-ROM Link
Shakespeare, "Full Fathom Five": Is the sea deadly or purifying? Do other poems on this list concern a "sea change" of some sort?
Cowper, "The Castaway"
C. Smith, From "Beachy Head"
Tennyson, "Crossing the Bar"
Whitman, "Out of the Cradle Endlessly Rocking": Why does the child's initiation into some sort of poetic calling take place at the seashore? Compare Whitman's treatment of the seashore in "Song of Myself," section 11 ("Twenty-eight young men bathe by the shore").
Arnold, "Dover Beach": Compare Arnold's treatment of the sea in "To Marguerite."
Lanier, "The Marshes of Glynn"
Hardy, "The Convergence of the Twain"
Frost, "Neither Out Far Nor In Deep"
E. Thomas, "As the team's head brass"
Stevens, "The Idea of Order at Key West"
Williams, "The Yachts"
Moore, "The Fish": This poem appears to be describing the sea-life, but turns to contemplate the paradox of the sea bringing life to the cliff it erodes. Have your students locate the turn and ask them whether the poem is really about the fish.
Eliot, "The Dry Salvages"
Bogan, "Night"
Warren, "Masts at Dawn"
Bishop, "The Moose"
Swenson, "Goodbye, Goldeneye"

R. S. Thomas, "Welsh Landscape" and "The View from the Window"
Clampitt, "The Sun Underfoot Among the Sundews"
Guest, "Twilight Polka Dots"
Rich, "Diving into the Wreck" *CD-ROM Link
Momaday, "Headwaters"
Hass, "Tahoe in August"
Boland, "That the Science of Cartography Is Limited" *CD-ROM Link

16.3 Flowers and Trees

Spenser, *The Faerie Queene*, Book 1 (stanzas 8 & 9)
Herrick, "To Daffodils"
Herbert, "The Flower"
Waller, "Song ('Go, lovely rose!')"
Elliot, "The Flowers of the Forest"
Blake, "The Sick Rose"
Emerson, "The Rhodora"
Thoreau, "I Am a Parcel of Vain Strivings Tied"
Tuckerman, From *Sonnets, Second Series*
Frost, "Birches" and "Design"
A. Lowell, "The Weather-Cock Points South"
Lawrence, "Bavarian Gentians"
W. C. Williams, "Asphodel, That Greeny Flower"
Moore, "Nevertheless"
Warren, "Bearded Oaks"
Page, "Deaf-Mute in the Pear Tree"
Clampitt, "Beethoven, Opus 111"
Wilbur, "Seed Leaves"
Larkin, "The Trees"
Atwood, "Flowers"
Graham, "Opulence"
Erdrich, "I Was Sleeping Where the Black Oaks Move"

16.4 Animals

Writing about animals may challenge poets' powers of description and specificity, and test their abilities to describe nonhuman creatures on their own terms. You might ask students to consider the degree to which these poems turn animals into people: when a poem carefully delineates and characterizes an animal, does it necessarily treat the animal as though it were human? What kind of knowledge about animals can poets provide that zoology cannot? The tendency of animal poems to shift into moral reflections, in the manner of Aesop's fables, makes them useful for teaching poetic closure. How may writing about animals free poets from some of the constraints of decorum? What liberties of language may poets wish to take in order to capture these creatures so like and yet so unlike ourselves?

Lovelace, "The Grasshopper": How does Lovelace keep this from being the Aesopian prodigal grasshopper (the one who wouldn't listen to the frugal ant)?

Taylor, "Upon a Spider Catching a Fly": From the minutely observed details of the first five stanzas, could we have predicted the turn to the moral lesson of the last five? What is the effect of the closing shift in man-animal comparisons from man as wasp caught in the devil's net to man as nightingale?

Gray, "Ode (On the Death of a Favorite Cat, Drowned in a Tub of Goldfishes)": Compare Gray's flip moral to Taylor's more studied one. To what degree is the difference dependent on the way Taylor compares human beings to animals, while Gray turns his animals into human beings? Compare both poems with others in this group (by Blake, Burns, Clare, Melville) that stress the savagery of animals.

Smart, "Jubilate Agno," lines 697–770 ("For I will consider my Cat Jeoffry"): How does Smart manage so exact an inventory of "complete cat" (line 744), while all the time interpreting the cat's activities as worshipful, and in that sense as human and not catlike? What is the effect of devoting a complete line to each action of the cat? Is there a narrative or some other principle of order to the sequence of activities Smart describes? This is a good text with which to focus on the language of animal poems. Smart's cat "camels his back" (line 755): what other unusual verbs does Smart introduce? A class exercise could emerge from this question: point out that names of some animals are conventionally used also as verbs (dog, fox, badger), and ask students to invent new idioms on the model of these or Smart's: what would it mean to "cat"? to "lamb"? to "spider"?

Blake, "The Lamb" and "The Tyger": As line 17 of "The Lamb" tells us, this poem is spoken by a child. For this child, is the lamb a real, living creature, or a religious emblem? Who speaks in "The Tyger"? Line 20 asks what is probably the best question for thinking about the two poems together.

Clare, "Badger": What accounts for the dispassionate tone in which this violent encounter is set forth? How does Clare shape our feelings about the savagery of the badger and of the men who hunt him? Why do men enjoy the badger's savagery as a display or sport? What happens when a creature from the wild is brought into the town?

Melville, "The Maldive Shark": Is this a pilot-fish's-eye view of the shark? If this were one of Aesop's fables, what would the moral be? Why doesn't Melville draw a moral? or does he?

Whitman, "A Noiseless Patient Spider": Compare to Taylor's, "Upon a Spider Catching a Fly"; in each poem, what is signified by the spider's ability to spin his web out of himself? Compare to Shelley's "To a Skylark"; how do Whitman and Shelley make animals into figures for their own poetic aspirations? A class exercise: complete Tennyson's "The Eagle" and Melville's "The Maldive Shark" with a Whitmanian ending, a comparison between the animal and the poet, perhaps starting with "And you, O my soul. . . ." In which case are the results a parody of Whitman?

Dickinson, #986 ("A narrow Fellow in the Grass"): This poem is like a riddle; the answer is "a snake." Students will have other guesses, though, and it can be useful to list the clues that allow us to zero in on the identification of this ordinary and yet mysterious creature. Why does Dickinson, like Shelley in "To a Skylark," describe the snake largely in terms of things that are like it? Why is this snake frightening? Can a poet write about a snake without invoking the story of the serpent in the Garden of Eden?

Williams, "Poem": Compare Williams's short, enjambed lines and Smart's long, end-stopped ones (in "Jubilate Agno," above) as two methods of representing the way cats move. Williams's title suggests that his version is also about the way poems move.

Lawrence, "Snake": Compare to Dickinson's poem #986 ("A narrow Fellow in the Grass"). Lawrence's poem might also be studied in the context of a number of poems centering on an unexpected encounter between a person and an animal, including Frost's "The Most of It" and the selections listed below by Bishop and Nemerov.

Moore, "The Fish": Compare with Bishop's poem below. Both poems begin in precise, imagistic details and end in epiphanies that suggest issues far larger than the subjects at hand, but how does Bishop's poem find transcendence in endurance differently than does Moore's?

Millay, "The Buck in the Snow"

Birney, "Slug in Woods"

Bishop, "The Fish" and "The Moose"

Lowell, "Mr. Edwards and the Spider"

Nemerov, "The Goose Fish": What is the function of the closing mention of the zodiac, with its constellations representing animals (including Pisces, the fish)?

T. Hughes, "Pike"

Ammons, "Silver"

Zarin, "The Ant Hill"

16.5 Birds

In their capacity to sing and to soar, birds often figure as some version of poets, and poems about birds tend to be meditations on the art of poetry itself. Why do these poetic birds tend to grow less melodious in the twentieth century?

Skelton, "Phillip Sparow"

Shelley, "To a Skylark": Compare the advantages over mankind that Shelley attributes to the skylark with those that Burns attributes to his creature in "To a Mouse." How does Shelley's series of likenesses for the skylark depend on the poet's not being able to see it, but only to hear its song? Which other poems in this list or in section 16.4, "Animals," delineate an animal by asking it, at least implicitly, "What is most like thee"?

Keats, "Ode to a Nightingale"

Poe, "The Raven"

Tennyson, "The Eagle": Although the poem gives the eagle "hands" and enables him to "stand," this bird does not seem to be turned into a person. Why not?

Dickinson, #328 ("A Bird came down the Walk—") and #1463 ("A Route of Evanescence"): In the first poem, what kinds of observations does Dickinson make when the bird is unaware of her? How does her knowledge—and her language—about the bird change when the bird becomes aware of her presence? How close does the speaker get to the bird in other poems in this group, and with what differences in effect? Sending "A Route of Evanescence" to a friend, Dickinson wrote, "Please accept a Humming Bird." Your students may suggest other possible answers to this riddle. What characteristics of hummingbirds make this cryptic poem suited to them?

Hardy, "The Darkling Thrush": On the eve of the twentieth century, the poet hears a diminished version of those lush birdsongs of the English literary tradition. Hardy's original title for this poem was "By the Century's Death-Bed." Does the poem end on a note of hope or gloom? Compare the bleak landscape against which this thrush sings to the landscape in which Keats's nightingale sings.

Hopkins, "The Windhover"

Frost, "The Oven Bird" and "Never Again Would Birds' Song Be the Same"

Stevens, "Thirteen Ways of Looking at a Blackbird"

Warren, "Evening Hawk"

Kunitz, "Robin Redbreast"

Swenson, "Goodbye, Goldeneye"

Van Duyn, "Letters from a Father"
MacPherson, "The Swan"
Momaday, "The Eagle-Feather Fan"

16.6 Seasons and Seasonal Change

Poems about seasonal change lend themselves to meditation on mortality (**Hopkins**), on the genuine necessities of life in the face of the years' ravages (**Lovelace**), and on the mystery of change in nature or in oneself (**Dickinson**). Conversely, seasonal change, because of its cyclic nature, can also symbolize endurance or the conflation of memories from many years into an almost timeless singularity (**Zarin**).

Lovelace, "The Grasshopper"
Dickinson, #1540 ("As imperceptibly as Grief")
Hopkins, "Spring and Fall"
Snodgrass, From *Heart's Needle*, 10 ("The vicious winter finally yields")
Hass, "Tahoe in August"
Zarin, "The Ant Hill"

A. *Spring and Summer*

Anonymous, "The Cuckoo Song"
Chaucer, "The General Prologue": Compare to the opening lines of Eliot's *The Waste Land*. As an exercise, have your students characterize the spring as they know it; to make the exercise more valuable, combine it with an exercise in the study of versification, by asking them to choose a meter or stanza form. This also provides a good opportunity to introduce the concept of "pathetic fallacy": point out how April rain can effectively figure as either delightful or horrific depending entirely on the mood of the poet and poem.
Surrey, "The Soote Season"
Shakespeare, Sonnet 18 ("Shall I compare thee to a summer's day?") and "It Was a Lover and His Lass"
Nashe, "Spring, the Sweet Spring"
Donne, "Good Friday, 1613. Riding Westward"
Herrick, "Corinna's Going A-Maying"
Tennyson, "In Memoriam A. H. H.," section 95 ("By night we lingered on the lawn")
R. Browning, "Home-Thoughts, From Abroad"
Swinburne, "When the Hounds of Spring Are on Winter's Traces"
Housman, "Loveliest of Trees, the Cherry Now"
Frost, "The Oven Bird"
Stevens, "Sunday Morning" (*CD-ROM Link) and "Peter Quince at

the Clavier": How does Stevens make spring a symbol of both rebirth and ageless endurance? Can we explain the logic behind his paradox? These questions might be useful when teaching paradox itself (see section 5.4).

Eliot, *The Waste Land*
Cummings, "Spring is like a perhaps hand"
Clampitt, "The Sun Underfoot Among the Sundews"
Larkin, "The Trees"
Snodgrass, From *Heart's Needle*, 2 ("Late April and you are three; today")
Snyder, "Above Pate Valley"

B. Fall and Winter

In some of these poems, winter's barrenness and sterility may spur the imagination (**Hecht**), or may draw the human community closer together (**Campion, Frost's** "The Wood-Pile"); in others it isolates the individual from the community, or seems a harbinger of death (**Dickinson, Frost's** "Stopping by Woods on a Snowy Evening"). Winter may be as much a spiritual state—a "mind of winter," in the words of *Stevens's* "The Snow Man"—as a state of nature (**Hardy**), or a time of life as well as a time of year (**Shakespeare's** Sonnet 73).

Anonymous, "The Seafarer"
Shakespeare, Sonnet 73 ("That time of year thou mayst in me behold") and "Blow, Blow, Thou Winter Wind"
Campion, "Now Winter Nights Enlarge"
Thomson, "Winter"
Coleridge, "Frost at Midnight"
Shelley, "Ode to the West Wind"
Keats, "To Autumn"
Emerson, "The Snow-Storm"
Longfellow, "The Cross of Snow"
Whitman, "To a Locomotive in Winter"
Dickinson, #258 ("There's a certain Slant of light")
Hardy, "The Darkling Thrush"
Yeats, "The Wild Swans at Coole"
Frost, "The Wood Pile" and "Stopping by Woods on a Snowy Evening"
Stevens, "The Snow Man"
Millay, "The Buck in the Snow"
Graves, "To Juan at the Winter Solstice"
Hayden, "Those Winter Sundays"
C. K. Williams, "Snow: II"
Kenney, "Apples on Champlain"

16.7 The Skies

A. *Night Skies*

Sidney, *Astrophil and Stella*, 31 ("With how sad steps, O moon, thou climb'st the skies")
Jonson, "Queen and Huntress"
Taylor, "Meditation 8 ('I kenning through astronomy divine')": How does Taylor use the knowledge of astronomy as a device to excite the reader's interest in looking toward heaven?
Keats, "Bright Star"
Whitman, "When I Heard the Learn'd Astronomer"
Meredith, "Lucifer in Starlight"
MacNeice, "Star-gazer"
Larkin, "Sad Steps"

B. *Wet and Rough Weather*

Anonymous, "The Seafarer"
Anonymous, "Western Wind"
Anonymous, "Sir Patrick Spens" *CD-ROM Link
Swift, "A Description of a City Shower"
Blake, "The Sick Rose"
Shelley, "Ode to the West Wind"
Emerson, "The Snow-Storm"
Poe, "The Raven"
Hardy, "During Wind and Rain"
W. C. Williams, "The Red Wheelbarrow"
MacNeice, "London Rain"
C. K. Williams, "Snow: II"

16.8 Farms and Rural Life

Blurring the opposition of nature and society, poems of farming life are not necessarily nostalgic and are rarely filled with the rapture of being outdoors and away from the town. They combine elements of daily hardship, death, birth, brutality, suffering, joy, weather, beauty, ugliness, and banality. Their flora and fauna are usually domesticated and their gardens are gardens of toil more often than of tranquility. (See also section 12.1, " 'Peasant' and 'Blue-Collar' Poets.")

Burns, "To a Mouse"
Housman, "Is My Team Ploughing"
Robinson, "Miniver Cheevy"
Frost, "Mending Wall," "The Hill Wife," and "Directive"

E. Thomas, “As the team’s head brass”
W. C. Williams, “The Red Wheelbarrow”
Lawrence, “Love on the Farm”
Toomer, “Reapers” and “Harvest Song”
Kavanagh, From “The Great Hunger”
Page, “Deaf-Mute in the Pear Tree”
Clampitt, “Beethoven, Opus 111”
Murray, “Noonday Axeman”
Heaney, “Digging”
Komunyakaa, “Banking Potatoes”
Kenney, “Apples on Champlain”
Muldoon, “Gathering Mushrooms”

CHAPTER 17

Gender Relations

17.1 Love

Like nature, romantic love never goes out of fashion as a topic in poetry, and any number of possible groupings of poems could make a good lesson in reading love poetry. The general list below illustrates the range of tones and approaches to the subject; the more specific lists that follow gather poems centering on seduction, fidelity and infidelity, farewells and absences, sex, and marriage. (See also section 4.1.B, "Love Sonnets.")

Anonymous, "Alison"
Anonymous, "Western Wind"
Anonymous, "There Is a Lady Sweet and Kind": Compare to other poems in this group that praise the beloved (Byron, Cummings, Roethke)
Wyatt, "The Long Love, That in My Thought Doth Harbor"
Surrey, "Love, That Doth Reign and Live Within My Thought"
Spenser, *Amoretti*
P. Sidney, *Astrophil and Stella*
Daniel, "Delia"
Shakespeare, Sonnets
Donne, "The Good-Morrow"
Jonson, "Though I Am Young and Cannot Tell"

Wroth, From "A Crowne of Sonnets Dedicated to Love"
Herbert, "Love (III)"
Marvell, "The Definition of Love"
Blake, "The Garden of Love"
Byron, "She Walks in Beauty"
Cummings, "somewhere I have never travelled, gladly beyond": Could this poem be spoken by a man or a woman, to a man or a woman?
Graves, "Love Without Hope"
Roethke, "I Knew a Woman"
Snyder, "Four Poems for Robin"

A. *Seduction*

The coy lady of Renaissance lyric called upon all the inventive allurements of the passionate lover. Most of the poems on this list employ some version of the *carpe diem* motif, advising the woman to "seize the day" and yield to her suitor before her youth and charms fade and she is no longer desirable. Questions of love and mortality are thus curiously intertwined in a number of poems in the Renaissance tradition of seduction lyrics. How can we reconcile the picture of women presented in these poems—as unyielding and in need of elaborate persuasions to love—with the frequent suggestion in poems in the next group ("Fidelity and Infidelity") that women are loose and faithless? On the model of **Ralegh's** parodic "reply" to **Marlowe's** shepherd, or of **Parker's** "One Perfect Rose," you might have students frame the woman's response to some of the poems in this list.

Queen Elizabeth I, "When I Was Fair and Young" *CD-ROM Link: What is the price of being a coy mistress, according to this poem?
Spenser, *Amoretti*, Sonnet 67 ("Lyke as a huntsman after weary chace")
Marlowe, "The Passionate Shepherd to His Love" *CD-ROM Link: The effectiveness of the shepherd's ploys may be judged by reading along with this poem Ralegh's "The Nymph's Reply to the Shepherd" and Lewis's modern rendition, "Song ('Come, live with me and be my love')" *CD-ROM Link
Shakespeare, "Oh Mistress Mine"
Campion, "My Sweetest Lesbia"
Donne, "The Flea"
Jonson, "Song: To Celia (I)"
Herrick, "Corinna's Going A-Maying" and "To the Virgins, to Make Much of Time"
Waller, "Song ('Go, lovely rose!')
Marvell, "To His Coy Mistress"
Behn, "The Disappointment"

Finch, "Adam Posed"
Gay, Songs from *The Beggar's Opera*, "Air XVI"
Goldsmith, "When Lovely Woman Stoops to Folly": A useful reminder that if the woman does seize the day, she may be subject to social censure, as the man is not.
Eliot, *The Waste Land*: Compare the dreary seduction of the typist by the clerk ("He makes a welcome of indifference") and its aftermath to Behn's "The Disappointment" and Goldsmith's "When Lovely Woman Stoops to Folly."
Parker, "One Perfect Rose"
Cummings, "since feeling is first": What devices of Renaissance seduction poems does Cummings rework? What is the effect of the Renaissance flavor of the vow "lady I swear by all flowers"?
Jarrell, "A Man Meets a Woman in the Street"
Hecht, "The Ghost in the Martini"

B. *Fidelity and Infidelity*

Anonymous, "The Unquiet Grave" and "Bonny Barbara Allan"
Wyatt, "They Flee from Me" *CD-ROM Link
P. Sidney, *Astrophil and Stella*, 90 ("Stella, think not that I by verse seek fame")
Shakespeare, Sonnet 116 ("Let me not to the marriage of true minds")
Donne, "Woman's Constancy," "The Anniversary," "The Funeral," and "The Relic"
Wroth, "Song ('Love a child is ever crying')"
Carew, "Song. To My Inconstant Mistress"
Suckling, "Song ('Why so pale and wan, fond lover?')"
Behn, "Song ('Love Armed')"
Burns, "John Anderson, My Jo" and "A Red, Red Rose"
Byron, "When We Two Parted"
Keats, "La Belle Dame sans Merci"
W. C. Williams, "Asphodel, That Greeny Flower"
Bogan, "Juan's Song"
Larkin, "An Arundel Tomb"
C. K. Williams, "Snow: II"

C. *Farewells and Absences*

Chaucer, "Cantus Troli" from *Troilus and Criseide*
Wyatt, "The Lover Showeth How He Is Forsaken of Such as He Sometime Enjoyed" ("They Flee from Me") *CD-ROM Link
Drayton, "Idea," 61 ("Since there's no help, come let us kiss and part")

Donne, "Song ('Sweetest love, I do not go')," "A Valediction of Weeping," and "A Valediction Forbidding Mourning" *CD-ROM Link
Bradstreet, "A Letter to Her Husband, Absent upon Public Employment"
Lovelace, "To Lucasta, Going to the Wars"
Gay, Songs from *The Beggar's Opera*, "Air XXII"
Byron, "So We'll Go No More A-Roving"
Longfellow, "The Cross of Snow"
Brontë, "Remembrance"
Melville, "Monody"
A. Lowell, "Patterns"
Auden, From "Twelve Songs," "IX [Funeral Blues]"
MacNeice, From "Autumn Journal ('September has come and I wake')"
Bishop, "One Art"
Berryman, Dream Songs 145 ("Also I love him; me he's done no wrong")
Douglas, "Vergissmeinnicht"
Creeley, "Bresson's Movies"
Snodgrass, "Mementos"
Jennings, "My Grandmother"
Strand, "The Prediction"
Glück, "The Garden"
Kenney, "Aubade"

D. Sex

The topic of sex is not entirely divorced from the topic of love, of course, and some of the poems in one list might with equal pertinence be listed in the other. Asking students to categorize some of these poems under either topic might lead to provocative discussions. Which poems in this list argue that sex is not a natural component of love but its enemy, or an activity that may or may not have anything to do with love (**Millay**)? Most of these poems see sex from the man's point of view; do the women on this list write about sex differently than the men do?

Shakespeare, Sonnet 129 ("Th' expense of spirit in a waste of shame")
Donne, "The Ecstasy" and "Elegy XIX. To His Mistress Going to Bed"
Herrick, "The Vine" and "Upon Julia's Breasts"
Blake, "The Garden of Love," "I Askéd a Thief," and "A Question Answered"
Byron, From *Don Juan*
Keats, "The Eve of St. Agnes": The sexual consummation—if it is

such—occurs in stanza 36. But the force of Keatsian sensuality is perhaps most strongly felt in the section on Madeline undressing (stanzas 23–27): the picture of Madeline unclasping her "warmed jewels one by one" is arguably more titillating than anything in the randy Elizabethans. (For a comparison with the brittle eroticism of a century earlier, glance at Belinda's dressing room in Pope's "The Rape of the Lock," Canto I, lines 121–48.)

Whitman, "Song of Myself," section 24 ("Walt Whitman, a kosmos, of Manhattan the son"): Perhaps compare with W. C. Williams's "Danse Russe," another kind of celebration of the poet's own body, though for Williams it is his separateness from others that inspires his private self-involved dance.

Dickinson, #249 ("Wild Nights–Wild Nights!")
Millay, "I, Being Born a Woman and Distressed"
Kinnell, "After Making Love We Hear Footsteps"
Mathews, "Histoire"
Adcock, "The Ex-Queen Among the Astronomers"
Fenton, "In Paris with You"
Lee, "Persimmons" *CD-ROM Link

E. *Parenting*

Bradstreet, "Before the Birth of One of Her Children"
Berryman, "A Sympathy, A Welcome"
Judith Wright, "Woman to Man"
Van Duyn, "Letters from a Father"
Snodgrass, From *Heart's Needle*
Kinnell, "After Making Love We Hear Footsteps"
Plath, "Morning Song"
Erdrich, "Birth"

F. *Marriage and Partnership*

Spenser, "Epithalamion"
Bradstreet, "To My Dear and Loving Husband" *CD-ROM Link
Meredith, From *Modern Love*
Jarrell, "A Man Meets a Woman in the Street"
Larkin, "Talking in Bed"
Snodgrass, "Mementos"
Jennings, "One Flesh"
Porter, "An Exequy"
Rich, "Aunt Jennifer's Tigers" and "Living in Sin"

Corso, "Marriage": Why is the self-pitying, whining voice of the speaker so appealing? Compare Corso's picture of marriage, as a social institution to which there is great pressure to conform, to Spenser's picture of it as a triumphal procession. Which poem is more candid about the sexual impulses that marriage legitimates?

Heaney, "The Skunk"

17.2 Gender Identity

A. *Being Female*

Bradstreet, "The Prologue"
Philips, "To My Excellent Lucasia, on Our Friendship"
Behn, "To the Fair Clarinda, Who Made Love to Me, Imagined More Than Woman"
Montagu, "A Receipt to Cure the Vapors"
Barbauld, "The Rights of Woman" *CD-ROM Link
Bishop, "In the Waiting Room"
Judith Wright, "Eve to Her Daughters"
Rich, From "Eastern War Time" and "Diving into the Wreck" *CD-ROM Link

B. *Being Male*

Berryman, Dream Song 145 ("Also I love him: me he's done no wrong")
Justice, "Men at Forty"
Baraka, "An Agony. As Now."

C. *Men as Topics in Poetry by Women*

Lanyer, From *Salve Deus Rex Judaeorum*
Bogan, "Man Alone"
Judith Wright, "Eve to Her Daughters"

D. *Women as Topics in Poetry by Men*

Dunbar, "In Prais of Wemen"
Anonymous, "Mary Hamilton"
Pope, "Epistle to Miss Blount"
Goldsmith, "When Lovely Woman Stoops to Folly"
Blake, "A Question Answered"
Hardy, "The Ruined Maid"
Yeats, "Adam's Curse"
Frost, "The Silken Tent"
Cummings, "the Cambridge ladies who live in furnished souls"

Campbell, "The Sisters"
MacNeice, From "Autumn Journal"
Jarrell, "A Man Meets a Woman in the Street"
Wilbur, "Piazza di Spagna, Early Morning"
Heaney, "Punishment"
Leithauser, "In Minako Wada's House"

CHAPTER 18

War, Politics, and Protest

18.1 War

The poems on this list touch on many aspects of war: saber-rattling preparatory patriotism (**Whitman's** "Beat! Beat! Drums!", **Cummings's** " 'next to of course god"); the daily life of the soldier (**Kipling, Rosenberg, Owen, Reed**); the death of individual soldiers (**Hardy's** "Drummer Hodge," **Yeats, Cummings, Jarrell**); the aftermath of the slaughter (**Melville, Whitman's** "Vigil Strange," **Sandburg, Tate**); war's effect, or lack of it, on the home front (**Levertov**). Curiously, the actual conflict itself seems rarely to be a poetic subject: how would you account for this?

Lovelace, "To Lucasta, Going to the Wars": Compare to Kipling's "Tommy": what do both poems suggest about the romantic illusions or social pressures that send young men to war?
Elliot, "The Flowers of the Forest"
Emerson, "Ode (Inscribed to W. H. Channing)"
Howe, "Battle-Hymn of the Republic"
Melville, "Shiloh"
Whitman, "Vigil Strange I Kept on the Field One Night" and "Beat! Beat! Drums!"

Hardy, "Drummer Hodge" and "Channel Firing"
Housman, "Epitaph on an Army of Mercenaries": Compare to MacDiarmid's harsher rejoinder, "Another Epitaph on an Army of Mercenaries"
Kipling, "Tommy" and "Recessional"
S. Crane, From "War is Kind"
Sandburg, "Grass"
Edward Thomas, "As the team's head brass"
Sassoon, " 'They' "
Rosenberg, "Break of Day in the Trenches"
MacDiarmid, "Another Epitaph on an Army of Mercenaries"
Owen, "Anthem for Doomed Youth," "Dulce et Decorum Est" (*CD-ROM Link), and "Strange Meeting"
Cummings, " 'next to of course god america i"
Tate, "Ode to the Confederate Dead"
Lewis, "Where are the War Poets?"
Hope, "Inscription for a War"
Jarrell, "The Death of the Ball Turret Gunner"
Douglas, "Vergissmeinnicht" and "Aristocrats"
Larkin, "MCMXIV"
Hecht, "The Book of Yolek"
Levertov, "Tenebrae" *CD-ROM Link
Henry Reed, "Lessons of the War"
Hecht, " 'More Light! More Light!' "
Walcott, "A Far Cry from Africa" *CD-ROM Link
Fenton, "Dead Soldiers"

18.2 Social and Political Protest

What special resources does poetry have to register resentment against injustice, corruption, war and violence, national policy, or the general malaise of civilization? Can a poem include or imply a reasoned political argument, or must it be merely an impassioned outcry of rage?

Askew, "The Ballad Which Anne Askewe Made and Sang When She Was in Newgate"
Ralegh, "The Lie"
Barbauld, "The Rights of Woman" *CD-ROM Link
Blake, "London" (*CD-ROM Link), "And Did Those Feet," and "England! Awake! Awake! Awake!"
Wordsworth, "London, 1802"
Shelley, "England in 1819"
Hardy, "Channel Firing": How does Hardy's poem give bite to the

cliché that something (in this case the guns of war) is "loud enough to wake the dead"?

Yeats, "Easter 1916" *CD-ROM Link
Jeffers, "Shine, Perishing Republic"
Cummings, "'next to of course god america i"
Hecht, "'More Light! More Light!'"
Rich, From "Eastern War Time"
Levertov, "Tenebrae" *CD-ROM Link
Seeger, "Where Have All the Flowers Gone?"
Boland, "That the Science of Cartography Is Limited" *CD-ROM Link
Dove, "Parsley" *CD-ROM Link

A. *The Fall of the Mighty*

The Massachusetts Bay Psalm Book, "Psalm 58"
Fenton, "Dead Soldiers"

18.3 Rich and Poor

Poetry is not written in a vacuum chamber sealed off from the facts of economic inequity. You might want to discuss with the class whether some of these poems exploit in some way the picturesque poverty of their subjects. Why do there seem to be more poems written about the poor than about the rich?

Chaucer, "Complaint to His Purse"
Langland, *Piers Plowman*
Whitney, "A Communication Which the Author Had to London, Before She Made Her Will"
Blake, "Holy Thursday (II.)"
Wordsworth, "Resolution and Independence"
Robinson, "Richard Cory"
Lawrence, "The English Are So Nice!": This can be a useful poem to teach in this group, as it captures the cadences and blindnesses of those who see themselves as privileged.
Eliot, "Sweeney Among the Nightingales"
MacNeice, "Bagpipe Music"
Brooks, "kitchenette building" and "Boy Breaking Glass"
Duffy, "Warming Her Pearls"

CHAPTER 19

Race and Ethnicity

See also section 12, "Poetry by Marginalized Groups."

19.1 Racial and Ethnic Identity

Wheatley, "To S. M., a Young African Painter, on Seeing His Works"
P. L. Dunbar, "Sympathy"
L. Hughes, "Dream Variations" and "Cross"
Cullen, "Heritage" and "Incident"
Brooks: Compare the broken window as a "cry of art" in "Boy Breaking Glass" to Baraka's suggestion, in "In Memory of Radio," that the (black?) poet's art is the ability to say "Let's Pretend."
Baraka, "In Memory of Radio"
Brathwaite, "Ancestors"
Walcott, "A Far Cry from Africa" *CD-ROM Link: Compare to Cullen's "Heritage." What question of identity is being presented in both poems?
Soyinka, "Telephone Conversation"
Lee, "Persimmons" *CD-ROM Link

19.2 Racial and Ethnic Relations

Blake, "The Little Black Boy"

Kipling, "Recessional": This celebration of British imperial power—won by dominating those whom the conquerors could conveniently label "lesser breeds without the Law"—can be an instructive poem to teach in the context of questions of race. For the self-serving voice of imperialism, or at least of racial chauvinism, laid bare, compare Lawrence's "The English Are So Nice!"

Brown, "Slim in Atlanta" and "Bitter Fruit of the Tree"

Cullen, "Incident"

Hayden, "Night, Death, Mississippi": Compare with Brown's "Bitter Fruit of the Tree."

Rukeyser, "Ballad of Orange and Grape"

Soyinka, "Telephone Conversation"

Duffy, "Warming Her Pearls"

19.3 History and Traditions of a People

Elliot, "The Flowers of the Forest"

Toomer, "Reapers"

L. Hughes, "The Weary Blues" *CD-ROM Link

Kavanagh, From "The Great Hunger"

R. S. Thomas, "Welsh Landscape"

Hecht, "The Book of Yolek"

Rich, From "Eastern War Time"

Brathwaite, "Ancestors"

Murray, "Noonday Axeman"

Heaney, "Digging"

Boland, "That the Science of Cartography Is Limited" *CD-ROM Link

Erdrich, "I Was Sleeping Where the Black Oaks Move"

CHAPTER 20

Faith and Religion

Anonymous, "The Bitter Withy"
Donne, Holy Sonnets
Crashaw, "A Hymn to the Name and Honor of the Admirable Saint Teresa"
Frost, "Directive"
Larkin, "Church Going"

20.1 God

Herrick, "To Find God"
Dickinson, #59 ("A little East of Jordan")
Gascoyne, "Ecce Homo"
Ted Hughes, "Theology"

20.2 Faith and Doubt

Anonymous, From *Pearl*
Askew, "The Ballad Which Anne Askewe Made and Sang When She Was in Newgate"
Spenser, *The Faerie Queene*, Book 1
Herbert, "Affliction (I)" and "The Collar
Milton, "When I Consider How My Light Is Spent"

Dickinson, #185 (" 'Faith' is a fine invention")
Stevens, "Sunday Morning" *CD-ROM Link
Heaney, From "Station Island"

20.3 Prayers and Entreaties

Cædmon's "Hymn"
Herbert, "The Altar" and "Prayer (I)"
Smart, "Psalm 58"
Dickinson, #49 ("I never lost as much but twice")

20.4 The Christian Calendar

Southwell, "The Burning Babe"
Donne, "Good Friday, 1613. Riding Westward"
Herbert, "Easter Wings"
Milton, "On the Morning of Christ's Nativity"

20.5 Clergy

Chaucer, "The Pardoner's Prologue and Tale" *CD-ROM Link
Browning, "The Bishop Orders His Tomb at Saint Praxed's Church" and "Fra Lippo Lippi"
Sassoon, " 'They' "

CHAPTER 21

Individual Existence

21.1 Memory

Vaughan, "They Are All Gone into the World of Light!"
Wordsworth, "Lines Composed a Few Miles Above Tintern Abbey"
W. C. Williams, "Asphodel, That Greeny Flower"
Lowell, "My Last Afternoon with Uncle Devereux Winslow": Do Lowell's recollections of an uncle who died while the poet was in his early childhood include intimations of his own mortality?
Jennings, "My Grandmother"
C. K. Williams, "Snow: II"
Soto, "Not Knowing"

21.2 Mind and Body

Donne, "The Ecstasy": How is the speaker's characterization of the relation between mind and body designed to further his goal of seduction?
Finch, "The Spleen"
Emerson, "Intellect"
Whitman, "Song of Myself," section 24 ("Walt Whitman, a kosmos, of

Manhattan the son"): Compare Whitman's devout worship of his own body ("The scent of these armpits aroma finer than prayer," line 525) to Hopkins's drive to spiritual perfection through bodily denial.

Brontë, "The Prisoner"
Stevens, "Of Mere Being"
Moore, "The Mind Is an Enchanting Thing"

21.3 Sleep and Dreams

Sleep can be an escape from unpleasant waking realities (**Daniel, Milton**), or a visionary state akin to poetic inspiration (**Coleridge, Keats**). Erotic dreams lead to a rude awakening in the selections by **Herrick, Milton,** and **Keats**.

Anonymous, From *Pearl*
Langland, *Piers Plowman*
Anonymous, "Weep You No More, Sad Fountains"
Daniel, "Delia," 49 ("Care-charmer Sleep, son of the sable Night")
Herrick, "The Vine"
Milton, "Methought I Saw"
Coleridge, "Kubla Khan" *CD-ROM Link
Keats, "Ode to a Nightingale" and "The Eve of St. Agnes"
Heaney, "A Dream of Jealousy"

21.4 Solitude

These poems present solitude in a number of ways: as utter isolation from all other beings (**Cowper, Arnold, Clare, Dickinson**), or as pensive serenity (**Milton, Yeats**), or as a perilously tempting wavering between the two (**Frost,** "Stopping by Woods").

Milton, "Il Penseroso"
Cowper, "The Castaway"
Wordsworth, "I Wandered Lonely As a Cloud
Clare, "I Am"
Arnold, "To Marguerite"
Dickinson, #303 ("The Soul selects her own Society—")
Yeats, "The Lake Isle of Innisfree"
Frost, "Stopping By Woods on a Snowy Evening" and "The Most of It"
Kavanagh, From "The Great Hunger"
Murray, "Noonday Axeman"

CHAPTER 22

Civilization

22.1 Art

Wheatley, "To S. M., a Young African Painter, on Seeing His Works"
Poe, "To Helen"
R. Browning, "My Last Duchess": How is the duke's view of art as a means of possessing women different from that of Browning's artist in "Fra Lippo Lippi"?
C. Rossetti, "In an Artist's Studio"
Yeats, "Adam's Curse"
Pound, "Portrait d'une Femme"
Ormond, "Cathedral Builders"
Creeley, "Bresson's Movies"
Tomlinson, "Farewell to Van Gogh"
Rich, "Aunt Jennifer's Tigers"
Daniel Hall, "Mangosteens"

22.2 Music

Poems about music often reflect on the musical powers of verse. What powers are attributed to music? What distinctions are made between instrumental and vocal music? Why are most of the singers in these poems women?

Campion, "When to Her Lute Corinna Sings"
Dryden, "A Song for St. Cecilia's Day"
Wordsworth, "The Solitary Reaper"
E. B. Browning, "A Musical Instrument"
R. Browning, "A Toccata of Galluppi's"
Stevens, "Peter Quince at the Clavier"
Lawrence, "Piano"
L. Hughes, "The Weary Blues" *CD-ROM Link
Clampitt, "Beethoven, Opus 111"
Larkin, "For Sidney Bechet"
Merrill, "The Victor Dog": Is modern technology a substitute for the memory in which Wordsworth could preserve a song after it was heard no more ("The Solitary Reaper")?

22.3 Science

Cavendish, "Of Many Worlds in This World"
Poe, "Sonnet—To Science"
Whitman, "When I Heard the Learn'd Astronomer"
Dickinson, #185 ("'Faith' is a fine invention") and #861 ("Split the Lark—and you'll find the Music—")
Millay, "Euclid Alone Has Looked on Beauty Bare"
Schnackenberg, "Darwin in 1881"

A. *Enumeration*

Poems in which specific sums are counted or amounts are calculated present an interesting series of issues about the differences between the kinds of claims poetry and science make. What could be more prosaic than an arithmetical sum? Yet in "Loveliest of Trees" **Housman** manages to subtract twenty from seventy and come up with the right answer, and in section 11 of "Song of Myself" **Whitman** specifies that he is concerned with exactly "[t]wenty-eight young men." What is the effect of this numerical specificity, and why is it something we generally do not expect from poems? Why does a ballad about "The Three Ravens" seem to name the right number for a poem to be able to count, but a poem called, say, "The Thirty-three Ravens" might veer toward parody? (And yet **Yeats** can count fifty-nine swans with no parodic intent.) Questions of diction arise here as well, and you might compare the way poems indicate large amounts of things or vast distances, and the way science does (what could be a more poetic unit of measurement than a "light year"?).

Anonymous, "Mary Hamilton": The subtraction of one from four in the final stanza reveals a surprise; in light of this little arithmetic problem, is it merely coincidence that the poem (like most ballads) alternates lines of four and three beats?

Suckling, "Out upon It!": How is it characteristic of this speaker to think small numbers are something to make a fuss over ("three whole days") and big numbers something to be tossed off lightly ("a dozen dozen")?

Marvell, "To His Coy Mistress": Note especially lines 13–16: how do these vast sums of years distributed for various tasks of praise help to further the lover's suit?

Whitman, "Song of Myself," section 11 ("Twenty-eight young men bathe by the shore")

Housman, "Loveliest of Trees, the Cherry Now"

Yeats, "The Wild Swans at Coole": How does the exact count of "nine-and-fifty swans" figure into the poet's summing of his own autumnal years? Note also the curious specificity of the "nine bean-rows" in Yeats's "The Lake Isle of Innisfree."

Stevens, "Thirteen Ways of Looking at a Blackbird"

22.4 The City

Poems of the city can reflect on the way the individual fates of the anonymous masses that populate the city are interwoven (**Swift, Blake, Whitman, MacNeice**), or on the utter isolation of the individual when surrounded by the dense populace of the city (**Eliot, Rich**). The city most frequently written of in this collection is London. You might therefore teach the theme of the city by teaching all the London poems together: **Whitney,** From A *Sweet Nosegay*; **Blake,** "London" (*CD-ROM Link); **Wordsworth,** "London, 1802"; **Eliot,** *The Waste Land*; **MacNeice,** "London Rain"; **D. Thomas,** "A Refusal to Mourn the Death, by Fire, of a Child in London." You might also wish to teach as a group the poems set in New York City and/or Boston, perhaps comparing them to the poems set in London.

Whitney, From A *Sweet Nosegay*, "A Communication Which the Author Had to London, Before She Made Her Will"

Swift, "A Description of a City Shower": Why does "City Shower" begin with an orderly prediction of the weather from various signs, but end with an undifferentiated flood?

Pope, "Epistle of Miss Blount": Is the city Miss Blount is reluctant to leave recognizably like the one in Swift's poems?

Blake, "London" *CD-ROM Link: How and why are the civic institutions of the church, war, marriage, and prostitution interdependent?

How can the "manacles" that these social institutions use to shackle the populace be "mind-forg'd"?

Wordsworth, "Composed Upon Westminster Bridge, September 3, 1802": What makes this view of the city as beautiful as a country landscape? What will happen to this effect when the sun rises over the still, "smokeless" city?

Whitman, "Crossing Brooklyn Ferry": Not about the city, but the sort of meditation possible only in crowds. Compare the multiplicity of people and sights Whitman lists to the hodepodge of Swift's city.

Sandburg, "Chicago"

Pound, "In a Station of the Metro": Contrast with Wordsworth's "Westminster Bridge," where the city is compared to a pastoral or rural site or landscape.

Eliot, "The Love Song of J. Alfred Prufrock," "Preludes," and *The Waste Land*

H. Crane, "Proem: To Brooklyn Bridge"

Hughes, "Theme for English B"

Auden, "As I Walked Out One Evening": Compare this ballad for the modern city to some of the popular ballads.

MacNeice, "Bagpipe Music": Compare to O'Hara's vision of New York City as a blitz of signs, brand names, and random pleasures in "The Day Lady Died"; "London Rain."

Rukeyser, "Ballad of Orange and Grape"

Brooks, "kitchenette building"

Lowell, "For the Union Dead"

O'Hara "The Day Lady Died"

Gunn, "A Map of the City"

Rich, "Living in Sin"

Atwood, "At the Tourist Center in Boston"

Pinsky, "The Street"

Fenton, "In Paris with You"

CHAPTER 23

Universal Mysteries

23.1 Chance and Destiny

This group of poems deals explicitly with large matters of the design or contingency of events and lives (issues so grand that many other poems raise them on some level). See also chapter 20, "Faith and Religion," and perhaps chapter 21, "Individual Existence."

George Meredith, "Lucifer in Starlight"
Hardy, "Hap" and "The Convergence of the Twain"
Frost, "The Road Not Taken" and "Design": In what sense is "Design" a miniaturized version of Hardy's "The Convergence of the Twain"?
Moore, "What Are Years?"
Ashbery, "Brute Image"
Christopher, "The Palm Reader"
Muldoon, "Gathering Mushrooms"

23.2 Death

Poems on mortality, mutability, and transience are included. You might compare poems that welcome death or that arrive at some acceptance of it

(**Nashe, Landor, Keats**) and those that resist or defy it (**Donne, Thomas, Berryman**). See also section 15.8, "Illness."

Donne, Holy Sonnet 10 ("Death, be not proud, though some have called thee")
Johnson, "The Vanity of Human Wishes"
Leapor, "Mira's Will"
Landor, "Dying Speech of an Old Philosopher"
Keats, "When I Have Fears"
E. Thomas, "In Memoriam [Easter 1915]"
Auden, From "Twelve Songs," "IX. Funeral Blues"
Berryman, Dream Song 145 ("Also I love him: me he's done no wrong")
D. Thomas, "Do Not Go Gentle into That Good Night"
Douglas, "Vergissmeinnicht"
Dufault, "A First Night"
Jennings, "My Grandmother"
Sexton, "The Truth the Dead Know"
Sissman, From "Dying: An Introduction," "IV. Path. Report"
Plath, "Lady Lazarus"

23.3 The World Beyond

Herrick, "The White Island, or Place of the Blest"
Marvell, "Bermudas" and "The Garden"
Philips, "Epitaph"
Barbauld, "Life"
Coleridge, "Kubla Khan" *CD-ROM Link
Blake, "And Did Those Feet"
Yeats, "The Lake Isle of Innisfree," "Sailing to Byzantium," and "Byzantium"
Stevens, "Waving Adieu, Adieu, Adieu"
Merrill, From *The Book of Ephraim*
Porter, "An Exequy"
Momaday, "Two Figures"
Strand, "The Prediction"
Atwood, "Flowers"

Index